CAMPAIGN 320

BRITTANY 1944

Hitler's Final Defenses in France

STEVEN ZALOGA

ILLUSTRATED BY DARREN TAN

Series editor Marcus Cowper

Osprey Publishing
c/o Bloomsbury Publishing Plc
PO Box 883, Oxford, OX1 9PL, UK
Or
c/o Bloomsbury Publishing Inc.
1385 Broadway, 5th Floor, New York, NY 10018, USA
E-mail: info@ospreypublishing.com

www.ospreypublishing.com

OSPREY is a trademark of Osprey Publishing Ltd, a division of Bloomsbury
Publishing Plc.

First published in Great Britain in 2018

© 2018 Osprey Publishing Ltd

A CIP catalogue record for this book is available from the British Library.

ISBN: PB: 9781472827371
            ePub: 9781472827388
            ePDF: 9781472827364
            XML: 9781472827395

18 19 20 21 22   10 9 8 7 6 5 4 3 2 1

Editorial by Ilios Publishing Ltd (www.iliospublishing.com)
Index by Zoe Ross
Typeset in Myriad Pro and Sabon
Maps by Bounford.com
3D BEVs by The Black Spot
Page layouts by PDQ Digital Media Solutions, Bungay, UK
Printed in China through World Print Ltd

Osprey Publishing supports the Woodland Trust, the UK's leading woodland
conservation charity. Between 2014 and 2018 our donations are being
spent on their Centenary Woods project in the UK.

To find out more about our authors and books visit
www.ospreypublishing.com. Here you will find extracts, author
interviews, details of forthcoming events and the option to sign up for
our newsletter.

AUTHOR'S NOTE

There are many disparities in the spellings of place names in Brittany due to
the differences between the French and Breton languages. This is evident
even in the name of the region – for example, Bretagne in French and
Breizh in Breton. In addition, US Army campaign maps sometimes had their
own peculiar names for certain locations.

For brevity, the traditional conventions have been used when referring to
military units. In the case of US units, 2/38th Infantry refers to the 2nd
Battalion, 38th Infantry Regiment. The US Army traditionally uses Arabic
numerals for divisions and smaller independent formations (8th Division,
743rd Tank Battalion); Roman numerals for corps (VIII Corps), spelled
numbers for field armies (Third US Army). In the case of German units, 2./
GR 919 refers to the 2nd Company, Grenadier-Regiment 919; II./GR 919
indicates the 2nd Battalion of Grenadier Regiment 919. German corps were
designated with Roman numerals such as XXV Armee Korps, but the
alternate version 25. AK is used here for clarity. Field armies were
designated in the fashion 7. Armee, but sometimes abbreviated in the
fashion AOK 7; the former style is used here.

Unless otherwise noted, all photos in this book are from official US sources
including the National Archives and Records Administration, US Army
Military History Institute, Library of Congress and US Army Patton Museum.

GLOSSARY

AOK	Armeeoberkommando: Army high command, abbreviation for a German field army
AR	Artillerie-Regiment
FJR	Fallschirmjäger-Regiment: Paratrooper regiment
Festung:	Fortress
FFI	Forces Françaises de l'Intérieur: combined French resistance organization
FTP	Franc-Tireurs et Partisans Français (aka FTPF); communist resistance movement
GFM	Generalfeldmarschall: field marshal
GMC	Gun Motor Carriage, often a tank destroyer
GR	Grenadier-Regiment
Heer	German army
HKAA	Heeres-Küsten-Artillerie-Abteilung, Army coastal artillery regiment
Kriegsmarine	German navy
KVA	Küsten Verteidigung Abschnitt: Coastal Defense Sector (divisions sized)
KVU	Küsten Verteidigung Untergruppe: Coast Defense Sub-group (regimental sized)
MAA	Marine-Artillerie-Abteilung: Navy artillery regiment
MKB	Marine Küsten Batterie: Navy coastal battery
MHI	Military History Institute, Army Historical Education Center, Carlisle Barracks, PA
NARA	National Archives and Records Administration, College Park, MD
OB West	Oberbefehlshaber West: High Command West (Kluge's HQ)
PaK	Panzerabwehr Kanone: Anti-tank gun
Russ.	Russisches (Russian); suffix in German unit designation for Russian Ost-truppen
SAS	Special Air Service; British special forces unit
SHAEF	Supreme Headquarters, Allied Expeditionary Force (Eisenhower's HQ)
SP	Self-propelled
StP	Stützpunkt, Strongpoint (company-sized)
Tobruk	A class of small bunkers with circular openings for a crew-served weapon
Wehrmacht	German armed forces
z.b.V.	zur besonderen Verwendung: SpeciAugust 30al Purpose

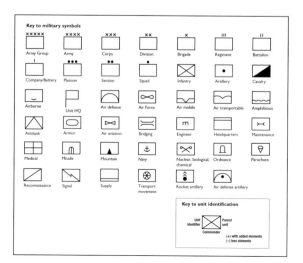

Key to military symbols

CONTENTS

INTRODUCTION

The plans for Operation *Overlord*, the Allied invasion of France in 1944, placed great emphasis on the need to capture deep-water ports in order to provide the logistical requirements of the advancing Allied armies. Cherbourg was liberated at the end of June 1944, but it had relatively modest docking facilities.[1] The *Overlord* plans focused on the requirement for the deep-water ports in Brittany, and in particular, Brest and the ports around the Quiberon Bay area, including Lorient and Saint-Nazaire. Brest was very familiar to US war planners, having been the major port of debarkation for the American Expeditionary Force in World War I. Following the Operation *Cobra* breakout in late July 1944, Patton's Third US Army was added to the Allied order of battle in Normandy. The primary mission of Patton's force was to race into Brittany and seize the vital Breton ports.

The subsequent race into Brittany in August 1944 was one of the fastest mechanized advances of the 1944 campaign. Within days, US units were on the doorstep of the ports of Brest, Saint-Nazaire and Lorient. Yet no sooner did Patton's Third US Army arrive in Brittany than doubts began to arise about the validity of its mission. The Germans had demolished the port facilities in Cherbourg in June 1944 and were likely to do the same in the Breton ports. This would cause months of delays in opening the ports. The collapse of the Wehrmacht in Normandy in August 1944 raised the issue of whether Patton's forces would be better employed heading eastward towards the Seine River and Paris. The capture of ports further east, notably Le Havre, Boulogne, and Antwerp, would be closer to the Allied front-lines and therefore more efficient from a logistical standpoint. In the event, only a single corps was left behind to lay siege to Brest while the rest of the Third US Army switched directions eastward in one of the most consequential developments of the summer campaign.

From Berlin's perspective, August 1944 was a month of defeat and despair. The Wehrmacht in Normandy was in retreat. Following the second D-Day – Operation *Dragoon* in southern France – Hitler authorized the withdrawal of the remaining German field armies in western, central and southern France. There was one exception. The garrisons of the Breton ports were declared to be "*Festung*" (Fortress), which in Hitler's vocabulary meant that they would be defended to the death.

Brest was subjected to a costly four-week siege operation in August–September 1944 before being liberated. Eisenhower decided against the waste of any troops to capture the other *Festung* ports, and they were to be

---

1 Steven Zaloga, Campaign 278: *Cherbourg 1944: The First Allied Victory in Normandy*, Osprey Publishing Ltd: Oxford, 2015.

left to rot on the vine. In the event, the French government began to petition Eisenhower to accelerate their liberation. Plans were initiated in early 1945 to liberate the *Festung* ports. This began in April 1945 at Royan on the Gironde estuary, but the heavy loss of civilian life led to a reconsideration of these schemes. The remaining *Festung* ports remained in German hands until after the capitulation of Nazi Germany in May 1945, remaining Hitler's last bastions in France.

The Breton ports were heavily fortified in 1943–44 as part of the Atlantic Wall program. This is an R699 gun casemate of 6./MAA 262 armed with a war-booty 152mm K15/16(t) gun near the Phare du Portzic lighthouse on the coast southwest of Brest.

CHRONOLOGY

1944

June 6	D-Day invasion of Normandy.
June 15	Middleton's VIII Corps activated in France.
June 18	SAS Camp Dingson is attacked and cleared by German security forces.
July 25	Operation *Cobra* break-out begins.
July 28	7. Armee orders the 84. Armee Korps to withdraw.
July 28	VIII Corps liberates Coutances.
July 31	Armored spearheads of VIII Corps in Avranches.
August 1	Patton's Third US Army activated in France.
August 1	4th Armored Division secures bridges near Avranches and Pontaubault.
August 1	4th Armored Division reaches Rennes, capital of Brittany.
August 2	BBC broadcasts the signal to initiate full-scale guerilla war in Brittany.
August 2	Luftwaffe starts night bomber attacks on bridges around Pontaubault.
August 3	At 2300hrs, the German garrison in Rennes is authorized to retreat.
August 4	13th Infantry Regiment, 8th Division, liberates Rennes.
August 5	6th Armored Division encounters 2. Fallschirmjäger-Division around Carhaix and Huelgoat.
August 6	6th Armored Division reaches outskirts of Brest.
August 6	83rd Division begins attacking Saint-Malo
August 7	CCB 4th Armored Division reaches Lorient.
August 7	Operation *Lüttich* offensive stalls in Mortain.
August 12	Ramcke assigned as commander of Festung Brest.
August 13	4th Armored Division directed eastward towards the Seine River.

The principal army command in Brittany was 25. Armee Korps, led by **General der Artillerie Wilhelm Fahrmbacher**. His headquarters, originally based in Pontivy, retreated to Lorient in early August to avoid capture by the advancing American VIII Corps. Although Fahrmbacher had planned to shift the headquarters to Brest, this move never occurred. Due to the lack of adequate communications with the embattled *Festung* ports of Saint-Malo and Brest, Fahrmbacher played little role in the Brittany campaign in August–September 1944.

The lack of centralized control in Brittany meant that local commanders mainly undertook the conduct of the battle for Brittany. In the case of Festung Saint-Malo, this was **Oberst Andreas von Aulock**. He served as a young officer in the German Army during the Great War, was awarded the Iron Cross First and Second Class, and ended the war as the adjutant of the 102. Reserve-Infanterie-Brigade. He returned to the army in 1937 and at the outset of the war was the commander of II./Infanterie-Regiment 212 and was again decorated after the Polish and French campaigns. He became commander of Infanterie-Regiment 226 in late 1940 and was decorated with the German Cross in Gold on October 27, 1941 while leading this unit in Russia. He was severely wounded in November 1942, but returned to lead Grenadier-Regiment 226 in the Kuban fighting, being decorated with the Knight's Cross on November 6, 1943. He was appointed as Festungskommandant Saint-Malo on March 24, 1944 and was decorated with the Oak Leaves to the Knight's Cross for his stubborn leadership in the battle for Saint-Malo. He was popularly called the "Mad Colonel" by US troops for his extravagant behavior during and after the Saint-Malo fighting. He was brother to Gen.Maj. Hubertus von Aulock, who commanded the defenses outside Paris in August 1944.

The Festungskommandant for Brest was **Oberst Hans von der Mosel**. He was a decorated veteran of the Great War and had been awarded the Knight's Cross in August 1942 while leading Infantry-Regiment 548 in Russia. He was appointed to the Brest command on May 1, 1943.

The best-known commander in the Brittany campaign was **Generalleutnant Hermann Bernard Ramcke**. He first served in the Imperial German Navy starting in 1905 and was decorated with the Iron Cross and the Prussian Golden Merit Cross while serving in the Marine-Infanterie in Flanders during the Great War. In 1919, he served with German forces in the fighting in the Baltics.

He remained in the Reichswehr after the war, becoming an *Oberstleutnant* in 1937. He transferred from the army to the Luftwaffe's 7. Flieger-Division in 1940, and completed the paratroop jump qualification at age 51. As a result, he was one of the few senior commanders to have served in three branches of the Wehrmacht. He led Fallschirm-Sturm-Regiment 1 during the airborne operation on Crete in 1941. After being promoted to *Generalmajor*, he was assigned to the Fallschirmjäger-Brigade Afrika intended for the attack on Malta. This never transpired, and the unit, better known as the Ramcke Brigade, was sent to the Afrika Korps. The brigade won considerable fame after it was trapped and broke out of British encirclement. Ramcke was ordered back to Germany after this exploit and was personally awarded the Oak Leaves to the Knight's Cross by Hitler. He was subsequently appointed to command the 2. Fallschirmjäger-Division. He remained in command of the division in the opening phase of the Brittany campaign, and was ordered to take command of Festung Brest on the evening of August 12, 1944, with Mosel becoming his deputy commander. Generalmajor Hans Kroh took over command of the 2. Fallschirmjäger-Division. Ramcke's stubborn defense of Brest led to his decoration with the Swords and Diamonds to the Knight's Cross. In 1951 a French court convicted him of war crimes in connection to reprisals during the anti-partisan campaign in Brittany. Curiously enough, Maj. Gen. Troy Middleton testified in his defense during the trial, citing the proper behavior of his troops in the fighting for Brest. His imprisonment was brief due to the intervention of Konrad Adenauer's government. Adenauer may have come to regret this effort after Ramcke became notorious afterwards for his involvement in extreme nationalist politics in Germany.

AMERICAN COMMANDERS

Lieutenant-General George S. Patton led the Third US Army during the initial phase of the Brittany campaign. He strongly influenced the pursuit into Brittany by the two armored divisions, often prodding his corps commander,

BELOW LEFT
Lieutenant-General George Patton spent much of August 1944 flying in light liaison aircraft like this L-5 since his Third US Army command was scattered across northern France from Brittany to the Seine river. This photo was taken on August 26, 1944 when Patton was traveling between the XX Corps headquarters near Fontainebleu and XII Corps near Troyes.

BELOW RIGHT
VIII Corps commander, Maj. Gen. Troy Middleton

Troy Middleton, to ignore the risks and maintain the momentum of the chase. He was also instrumental in extracting the Third US Army from the Brittany campaign once he realized that the mission was a dead-end. He saw greater potential in an advance eastward to the Seine, and so focused his attention on this mission later in August 1944.

The principal American commander in Brittany was **Maj. Gen. Troy Middleton**, leader of VIII Corps. Middleton had entered the army as a private in 1909 and rose through the ranks to become the army's youngest regimental commander in World War I. Although he had retired before the outbreak of World War II to become a college administrator, he returned to the Army and commanded the 45th Division in Italy with distinction. Old for an American corps commander, the army chief of staff, George C. Marshall, remarked that he would "rather have a man with arthritis in the knee than one with arthritis in the head." When the issue of retirement was raised in 1944, Eisenhower quipped that he wanted him back in command even if he had "to be carried on a stretcher." Middleton was an infantryman to the bone, and had difficulties working under Patton. Where Middleton tended towards an infantryman's caution, Patton urged a cavalryman's boldness. At several points in the campaign, Middleton opted for the cautious, prudent

Maj. Gen. John Wood (center), commander of the 4th Armored Division, was instrumental in convincing Bradley (left) and Patton (right) that the two armored divisions in VIII Corps would be better used in the pursuit to the Seine. This particular photo was taken two months later in the Metz campaign.

Maj. Gen. Charles Gerhardt, commander of the 29th Infantry Division.

approach only to incur Patton's wrath. While Middleton was a very capable commander, it took Patton's oversight to ensure the speedy liberation of Brittany.

Middleton was blessed with some excellent divisional commanders. The 4th Armored Division commander, **Maj. Gen. John Wood**, was one of the pioneers of the US Army's armored force. He was the catalyst for the change in strategic direction of Patton's Third US Army in mid-August, and the first to argue that the Brittany mission should be abandoned in favor of a pursuit to the Seine. The commander in the neighboring 6th Armored Division, **Maj. Gen. Robert Grow**, would later be considered one of the best US armored division commanders, though the division's leadership had a rocky start in early August 1944. The 2nd Infantry Division was led by **Maj. Gen. Walter Robinson**, best known for his leadership of the division in the Ardennes campaign, where it blunted the northern spearhead of the German attack. The 29th Division was commanded by the controversial **Maj. Gen. Charles Gerhardt**. He was widely considered to be an overbearing martinet, but his vigorous and demanding leadership turned the 29th Division into one of the best of the National Guard divisions.

OPPOSING ARMIES

THE WEHRMACHT

Brittany was one of the most significant regions of occupied France for Germany, providing the Kriegsmarine with ports that offered access to the Atlantic. Brest, Saint-Nazaire, and Lorient all became major naval bases for the Kriegsmarine. They were an essential element in the U-boat war against Britain and 1,170 U-boat patrols were conducted from these ports. Due to their proximity to British air bases, the harbors saw extensive projects in 1940–42 for the construction of bomb-proof U-boat shelters. The British commando raid against the Saint-Nazaire dry docks in 1942 was one of the main catalysts for the subsequent Atlantic Wall program to defend the Breton coast against future raids. Berlin assumed that the Allies would consider Brittany an attractive invasion site due to its extensive port infrastructure, and as a result it was one of the centers of Atlantic Wall construction.[2] The strongpoints built during this program played an important role in many of the battles in Brittany in August–September 1944. The extensive Kriegsmarine defensive infrastructure at Brest included Marine-Artillerie-Abteilung 262, which included 38 major coastal guns in the 75mm to 280mm range, served by about 900 troops.

The value of the Breton ports for the Kreigsmarine decreased dramatically prior to D-Day due to aggressive Royal Navy actions as well as RAF Coastal Command raids along the coast. Operation *Kinetic* consisted of naval patrols and air actions intended to exploit the Kriegsmarine evacuation of the Breton ports as well as other ports on the Bay of Biscay. Brest was the home port of destroyer flotillas through 1943, but most were transferred back to Germany before D-Day with the last leaving in March 1944. The two S-Boat flotillas in Brest (4. and 5. Torpedobootsflottille) were mostly transferred to Cherbourg in

The *Festung* ports of Brittany were of vital strategic interest to the Kriegsmarine as its westernmost base for U-boat operations into the Atlantic. Most of the U-boats escaped prior to the US Army advance into Brittany. This Type IXC, *U-510*, returned from a 110-day trip to Japan, arriving back at Festung Saint-Nazaire on April 23, 1945 before the surrender of the base in May 1945.

2   Steven Zaloga, Fortress 63: *The Atlantic Wall (1): France*, Osprey Publishing Ltd: Oxford, 2007; Gordon Williamson, Fortress 3: *U-boat Bases and Bunkers 1940–45*, Osprey Publishing Ltd: Oxford, 2003.

Operation *Kinetic* was a Royal Navy and RAF Coastal Command effort in August 1944 to sweep the Kriegsmarine from the Breton ports and Bay of Biscay. This is gun-camera footage of a strike by rocket-firing Beaufighters of 236 and 404 Squadrons off the French coast near Le Verdon-sur-Mer against torpedo-boat *T.24* in the foreground and destroyer *Z.24* behind. The *Z.24* was sunk in this encounter on August 25, 1944.

March–April 1944. At the time of D-Day, there was only one S-Boat still in Brest and the only remaining surface warships were 36 mine-warfare ships and 16 small escort and patrol vessels. Brest was home port for the 1. and 9. U-Flotille as well as other units. Following D-Day, the submarine force was re-located to Norway with the last submarines departing in August and early September 1944. German naval losses in August 1944, due mainly to Operation *Kinetic*, included 12 U-boats, 11 large ships, two destroyers, one torpedo boat and 53 smaller vessels.

The numerous Royal Air Force bombing attacks on the Breton ports led to the deployment of large numbers of heavy Kriesgmarine Flak batteries. The 3. Marine-Flak-Brigade in Brest consisted of five battalions with about 80 heavy Flak guns and 120 light guns serviced by about 4,000 personnel.

Coastal Artillery in Brittany 1944

Kreigsmarine	Sector	Composition
MAA 608	Saint-Malo	3 batteries: 6 x 194mm; 4 x 105mm; 4 x 120mm
MAA 262	Brest	7 batteries: 4 x 150mm; 4 x 105mm; 4 x 75mm; 4 x 164mm + 4 x 75mm; 4 x 150mm; 3 x 88mm + 3 x 152mm; 4 x 280mm
MAA 264	Lorient	4 x 164mm + 2 x 150mm; 4 x 150mm; 3 x 340mm; 4 x 203mm
leMAA 683	Belle Ile	3 batteries: 2 x 75mm; 3 x 75mm; 4 x 105mm
leMAA 688	Belle Ile	3 batteries: 4 x 138mm; 2 x 75mm; 3 x 75mm
MAA 681	Ile de Groix	3 batteries: 4 x 105mm; 4 x 75mm; 4 x 75mm
MAA 280	Saint-Nazaire	5 batteries: 4 x 75mm; 4 x 105mm; 4 x 170mm; 2 x 240mm; 2 x 240mm
Heer	Sector	Composition
HKAA 1273	N. Brittany	2 batteries: 4 x 105mm; 4x 105mm
HKAA 1274	S. Brittany	2 batteries: 4 x 220mm; 4 x 105mm

The Atlantic Wall program added a substantial number of fortified strongpoints along the coast. These were divided into Coastal Defense Sectors (KVU: *Küsten Verteidigung-Abschnitt*). Each KVU was defended by a single infantry division, reinforced with army coastal artillery battalions (HKAA: *Heeres-Küsten-Artillerie-Abteilung*). In August 1944, Brittany had five of these sectors, but less than four divisions to man the strongpoints.

The Heer (Army) had a very substantial presence in Brittany on D-Day, but the force was gradually pilfered to reinforce the Normandy front in June and July 1944. The units in Brittany were subordinated to the 7. Armee under Gen. Paul Hausser, who also directed the divisions in Normandy. Prior to D-Day, the force in Brittany included three corps (25. Armee Korps, 74. Armee Korps, 2. Fallschirm Korps) and eight divisions. Of the roughly 200,000 troops in Brittany on D-Day, about 80,000 were sent to the Normandy front in June–July 1944.

By the time that the US Army pushed into Brittany at the beginning of August 1944, two of the corps headquarters had been sent to Normandy, leaving the 25. Armee Korps in overall command of Brittany. This corps was headquartered in Pontivy and previously had been responsible for western Brittany. On August 1, 1944, its order of battle included five divisions, though in reality, this was a hollow force. Most of the divisions were configured as static divisions (*Bodenständig*) which were intended for coastal defense on the Atlantic Wall. As a result, they had very limited mobility and tended to have a poor allocation of over-age or medically compromised troops. Most of the divisions were stripped of their better combat troops in June 1944 to form *Kampfgruppen* that were sent to the Normandy front. To make up for lost strength, the 25. AK assigned about a dozen *Ost* battalions to the divisions. These *Osttruppen* units were made up from former Soviet prisoners-of-war who volunteered for Wehrmacht service either for ideological reasons or simply to escape the lethal German POW camps. These turncoats were regarded with suspicion by most German infantry commanders and usually assigned to secondary coastal defense duties.

The 77. Infanterie-Division was a normal infantry division raised in January 1944 but never completely formed. Originally, it was deployed to the northeastern coast of Brittany around Saint-Malo. It was ordered to Normandy shortly after D-Day, and lost about a third of its infantry strength in two weeks of fighting on the Cotentin Peninsula during the Cherbourg campaign. On July 27, the remnants of the division were ordered to return to their original defensive role around Saint-Malo. To make up for their combat losses, the division was reinforced with two anti-partisan units, Ost-Bataillon 602 (Russ) and Sicherungs-Bataillon 1220. This division played a central role in the initial fighting around Avranches and Saint-Malo at the beginning of August 1944.

The 266. Infanterie-Division (Bodenständig) was stationed on the Côte du Nord. It was based on a two-regiment structure and had only about 8,900 troops on D-Day. The division formed Kampfgruppe Kentner to reinforce the Normandy front, which departed in mid-June, taking with it two infantry battalions, an artillery battalion, and most of the division's motor transport. A

The Quatre Pompes fortified submarine pens had been built at great cost in 1941–42 to shelter, replenish and repair the two U-boat flotillas operating out of Festung Brest until the summer of 1944. The Marineschule naval academy can be seen above it to the right. The command bunker for Festung Brest was located near the academy.

second, smaller *Kampfgruppe* was sent to Normandy late in June including one infantry battalion and an anti-tank gun battery. The division had been reduced to about 5,000 men by early August 1944.

The 343. Infanterie-Division (Bodenständig) was stationed on the western coast of Brittany around Brest from Brignogan to the southern base of the Crozon Peninsula. It was formed mainly from over-age and convalescent men. It formed Kampfgruppe Rambach for the Normandy front in June 1944, reducing its strength to about 8,000 troops by August 1944. It had two attached *Ost* battalions. This division was heavily involved in the fighting for Brest, primarily on the Armorique/Daoulas Peninsula and Crozon Peninsula.

The 265. Infanterie-Division (Bodenständig) had an initial strength of about 9,700 men in June 1944. Its Kampfgruppe Coep was sent to the Normandy front, depriving it of the equivalent of one infantry regiment and an artillery battalion, and leaving it with a total of about 6,100 men.

It was stationed on the southwest coast from the Bay of Douarnenez to Lorient. When the 275. Infanterie Division was sent to Normandy, the 265. Infanterie-Division took over its sector in the Saint-Nazaire area. It had three *Ost* battalions attached for coastal defense duty. The division saw little fighting in the 1944 fighting and withdrew into Festung Lorient and Festung Saint-Nazaire.

The 319. Infanterie-Division was the main occupation force on the Channel Islands. Although the 25. Armee Korps requested that it be transferred to Brittany in July 1944 for reinforcement, Hitler was adamant that it remain in place. As a result, it remained on the Channel Islands until the capitulation in May 1945 and did not see combat.

The reserve of the 25. Armee Korps was the 2. Fallschirmjäger-Division, undoubtedly the best combat formation in Brittany in August 1944. This was a veteran combat formation that was sent back to Germany from Russia in 1943–44 for reconstruction. It was an elite Luftwaffe formation with better quality recruits than any other division in Brittany. As in the case of the other divisions in Brittany, it shed its Fallschrimjäger-Regiment 6 to the Normandy front in June 1944, leaving it with only two paratrooper regiments. It was transferred to the Brest area from training grounds in Germany in mid-June, and took up positions to the northeast of Brest. The division was never fully deployed to Brittany. Fallschirmjäger-Regiment 2 lacked its I. Bataillon, which ended up fighting in the Operation *Market-Garden* battles in the Netherlands in September 1944. As will be described below, III./FJR 7 and one artillery battery were used to form Kampfgruppe Rochlewski in early August that took part in the fighting at Pontaubault Bridge and then in Saint-Malo. As a result, the division had only four of its nine paratrooper battalions at the time of the fighting in Brest. Although the I./FS-Artillerie Regiment 2 deployed to Brittany, its other two battalions did not. Fallschirm-Granatwerfer-Bataillon 2 also did not arrive. At the end of July, the division had a nominal strength of 7,551 men though in reality it never fought together at this strength due to this dispersal of its sub-formations.

The large number of Atlantic Wall bunkers and strongpoints in Brittany led to the deployment of Festungs-Stamm-Regiment 25. Headquartered in Pontivy under Oberst Witt, it numbered about 6,750 troops. Its three battalions manned the strongpoints around the major *Festung* ports of Brest, Lorient, and Saint-Nazaire. There were still some elements of Festungs-Stamm-Regiment 84 located in the bunkers of the Saint-Malo area after the 84. Armee Korps was transferred to Normandy.

One of the most common Flak guns in the Brest area was the Kriegsmarine 105mm SKC/33, a turreted weapon essentially identical to the warship gun except adapted for ground mounting. Each battery had four of these guns in addition to the associated fire-control equipment. This particular gun, a twin 105mm SKC/33 on double 88mm LC/31d mount was from 3./M.Fla.Abt. 811 near Kerédern, north of Brest. One of its guns and much of its turret armor has been blown off by artillery fire.

Without a doubt, the best German unit in Brittany was the 2. Fallschirmjäger-Division that took part in the defense of Festung Brest. These are three paratroopers captured during the fighting on September 9 wearing the distinctive Luftwaffe battledress.

Festung Brest had a *Landfront* defensive line with numerous strongpoints including this *Ringstand* on Rue Jean Jaurès near the junction with Rue du Vercors, part of the B216 strongpoint around the Place de Strasbourg. This *Ringstand* consisted of an underground bunker with a war-booty turret from a French Somua 35S tank. This was in the eastern part of the city assaulted by the 2nd Infantry Division. This photo was taken after the fighting by an Air Force team examining bomb damage.

German Order of Battle, Brittany, August 1944

Unit	Location	Commander
25. Armee Korps	Pontivy	Gen. der Art. Wilhelm Fahrmbacher
2. Fallschirmjäger-Division	Brest	Gen. der FS Hermann Bernard Ramcke
77. Infanterie-Division	St. Malo	Oberst Rudolf Bacherer
266. Infanterie-Division (Bodenständig)	Le Gollot	Gen.Lt. Karl Spang
343. Infanterie-Division (Bodenständig)	Brest	Gen.Lt. Erwin Rauch
265. Infanterie-Division (Bodenständig)	Redon	Gen.Lt. Walther Düvert
319. Infanterie-Division	Channel Islands	Gen.Lt. Rudolf Graf von Schmettow

The Luftwaffe was almost totally absent during the Brittany campaign, since most of its local strength had been drawn away into Normandy in June and July. As will be mentioned later, there were some bomber strikes early in the campaign against key bridge targets, conducted by squadrons based near Toulouse in southern France. During the siege of Brest there were a small number of airdrops of critical supplies conducted at night by Luftwaffe units.

THE US ARMY

Patton's Third US Army began to deploy to France in July 1944, but it was not formally activated until August 1, 1944. Until this point, Lt. Gen. Omar

A camouflaged M4 105mm assault gun of the 8th Tank Battalion, 4th Armored Division passes through Avranches on its way into Brittany on July 31. This version of the Sherman tank was fitted with a 105mm howitzer instead of the usual 75mm gun. It was intended to provide additional firepower to the tank battalions. Three assault guns were found in a platoon in the battalion headquarters company and one assault gun in each company headquarters for a total of six per battalion.

Bradey's First US Army had been a part of Gen. Bernard Montgomery's 21st Army Group. With two US field armies active in France in August 1944, Bradley was elevated to command the new 12th Army Group that included the First US Army and Patton's Third US Army.

The unit primarily associated with the Brittany campaign was Maj. Gen. Troy Middleton's VIII Corps. This corps had been activated on June 15, 1944 and had taken part in the Cherbourg campaign in June 1944 as part of the First US Army. It was attached to Patton's Third US Army on August 1, 1944 through September 4, 1944. When Patton's Third US Army was reoriented eastward in late August, VIII Corps became separated. As a result, it was reassigned again on September 5, 1944 to Maj. Gen. William Simpson's newly activated Ninth US Army. It remained part of this command through the battle for Brest. On October 4, 1944, VIII Corps was shifted from Brittany to the Ardennes, where it would play a critical role in the Battle of the Bulge six weeks later. The US forces remaining in Brittany after this were then placed under the 12th Army Group Coastal Sector command until March 25, 1945, when the newly arrived Fifteenth US Army arrived in the European Theater of Operations.

The VIII Corps had a variety of formations under its command in Brittany. At the outset of the campaign, it consisted of two infantry and two armored divisions. The 8th Infantry Division entered combat in Normandy on July 12, 1944, fighting the Battle of the Hedgerows. The 83rd Division entered combat on July 4, 1944, also during the Battle of the Hedgerows. Both of these divisions were part of the VIII Corps at this time, along with the 79th and 90th Divisions. When the VIII Corps was assigned to the Brittany mission at the end of July, the 79th and 90th Divisions were shed for the two armored divisions to permit a faster pursuit mission.

The 4th Armored Division was committed to combat on July 17, 1944 with VIII Corps, and the 6th Armored Division on July 27. Both of these divisions were in the 1943 light armored division configuration, which had a balanced force structure of three battalions each of tanks, armored infantry,

The VIII Corps was allotted a significant amount of heavy artillery to deal with the numerous fortified positions around Brest. This is an M1 155mm gun battalion on the road to Brest on August 18, 1944. The gun is being towed by a Mack NO 7-ton truck. There were two of these truck-towed battalions employed at Brest, the 559th and 561st Field Artillery Battalions.

and armored field artillery. US doctrine favored the use of armored divisions for pursuit and exploitation and their modest complement of infantry did not make them suitable for prolonged urban combat, as would become apparent in the Brittany campaign. They possessed only three infantry battalions compared to the nine infantry battalions in an infantry division.

With the exploitation mission completed in August, both armored divisions were sent eastward. The assault on Brest required more infantry, and so two additional divisions arrived to take their place, the 2nd Infantry Division on August 18 and the 29th Infantry Division on September 2. These

By D-Day, the old 37mm anti-tank gun used in infantry divisions had been replaced by the 57mm anti-tank gun, a copy of the British 6-pdr. This weapon was obsolete in the summer of 1944 when facing newer German tank types, but it was still useful as a direct fire support weapon when dealing with fortified positions. This is a 57mm gun of the anti-tank company of the 116th Infantry Regiment, 29th Infantry Division during the fighting in the Recouvrance area on the western side of Brest in September 1944.

were experienced divisions. For example, the 29th Division had suffered 12,000 casualties between its D-Day landings at Omaha Beach and the start of the siege of Brest in late August.

Besides the armored divisions, VIII Corps also had the 6th Armored Group attached. By this stage of the war, these group headquarters tended to have a more administrative than tactical role and their associated tank battalions were attached to infantry divisions on a semi-permanent basis. So the 2nd Infantry Division had the 741st Tank Battalion attached during the Brittany fighting and the 83rd Division had the 774th Tank Battalion; the 709th Tank Battalion was assigned as required. The VIII Corps also had 6th Tank Destroyer Group attached to manage its separate tank destroyer battalions. This headquarters was used to form Task Force A, since by this stage of war, the defensive role of these formations was no longer especially relevant to the battlefield circumstances.

In view of large amount of German fortifications around Brest, VIII Corps requested an unusually large field artillery force beyond the organic divisional artillery battalions. This eventually totaled five field artillery groups with 18 additional field artillery battalions. This included two 105mm howitzer battalions (one towed, one self-propelled); five 155mm howitzer battalions, five 155mm gun battalions (three towed, two self-propelled); two 8in. howitzer battalions; two 8in. gun battalions, and two 240mm howitzer battalions. These field artillery groups were used to provide reinforcing fire for the infantry divisions participating in the assault on Brest, as well as general support and counter-battery fire.

ABOVE LEFT
Besides the divisional field artillery battalions, each infantry regiment had a cannon company armed with six of these M3 105mm howitzers. This is Battery 6 of the cannon company of the 9th Infantry Regiment, 2nd Division on the outskirts of Brest on August 28, 1944.

ABOVE RIGHT
One of the lesser-known fire support weapons used by the US Army in 1944–45 was the "Four-deuce" 4.2in. mortar. These were deployed by corps-level chemical mortar battalions, each with 36 of these weapons. These fell under the Chemical Warfare Service since they were originally developed to fire smoke projectiles, a CWS weapon. However, a very effective high-explosive round was also available, and widely used by these units. This is a Four-deuce platoon in action outside Brest in September 1944.

VIII Corps	Maj. Gen. Troy Middleton
(Initial Brittany Campaign)	
8th Infantry Division	Maj. Gen. Donald Stroh
83rd Infantry Division	Maj. Gen. Robert Macon
4th Armored Division	Maj. Gen. John Wood
6th Armored Division	Maj. Gen. Robert Grow
(Siege of Brest)	
2nd Infantry Division	Maj. Gen. Walter Robinson
29th Infantry Division	Maj. Gen. Charles Gerhardt

THE FRENCH RESISTANCE

The French resistance consisted of a variety of small local militias, based around political parties, patriotic organizations, and military organizations. Resistance units were usually called Maquis; individual fighters were Maquisards. One of the most significant differences between Brittany and the rest of France was that the resistance movement was more unified due to the dominance of the communist Franc-Tireurs et Partisans Français (FTP or FTPF). The Bretons in the rural areas found the FTP's belligerent tactics more appealing than other groups that urged restraint until the Allies appeared.

De Gaulle's provisional government attempted to unify the various resistance groups under a common organization, the Forces Françaises de l'Intérieur (FFI), created on February 1, 1944. They were put under the army command of the État Major des FFI (EMFFI) led by Gen. Pierre Koenig which served as the formal link between the FFI and Eisenhower's SHAEF (Supreme Headquarters Allied Expeditionary Force).

Support for the FFI came from a variety of organizations. The British Special Operations Executive (SOE) had the oldest links to the French resistance, supplying personnel and equipment since the early days of the war. In the summer of 1944, the Special Air Service (SAS) sent teams into France to carry out missions as well as to provide a link to the FFI for expanded arms supply. The most significant of these in the Brittany campaign was Lt. Col. Lucien Bourgoin's 4 SAS, formed from the French 2e Régiment de Chasseurs Parachutistes. On the American side, the Office of Strategic Services (OSS) served as the equivalent of the SOE and its action arm was the Jedburgh teams which were small liaison groups, usually of mixed US, British, and French composition. The Special Forces Headquarters (SFHQ) was created on January 10, 1944 to coordinate US and British efforts – though in practice, the various "private armies" tended to operate independently. The BCRA (Bureau Centrale Renseignements d'Action: Central Bureau of Intelligence and Operations) was the primary French intelligence organization supporting the resistance movement. SHAEF attempted to direct most of the efforts in Brittany though Koenig's EMFFI.

A group of Breton Maquisards of an FTP unit on the Crozon Peninsula on August 21, 1944 riding on a captured German Feldwagen. They are armed with German 98k rifles and wear a mixture of civilian garb with bits of US military battledress.

OPPOSING PLANS

ALLIED PLANS

Brittany had played a significant role in the Allies' Operation *Overlord* plans due to the need for deep-water ports to support the land campaign. There were three major ports in Brittany, of which Brest was the most important. The ports of Saint-Nazaire and Lorient were also attractive, but Allied plans actually intended to develop Quiberon Bay into a major facility. *Overlord* anticipated that these ports would be in Allied hands by D+60 with a capacity of 37,000 tons per day to add to the 27,000 tons provided by the Mulberry harbor at Omaha Beach and the port of Cherbourg. The loss of the Mulberry harbor to a Channel storm in June 1944 made the capture of the Breton ports all the more urgent.

Some consideration was given to a second amphibious operation into Brittany in June or July 1944, due to the delays in breaking out from Normandy. This operation would have most probably used Patton's Third US Army. Three different scenarios were considered, Operation *Beneficiary* (Saint-Malo), Operation *Hands Up* (Quiberon Bay) and Operation *Swordhilt* (Brest). Atlantic Wall fortification was more extensive in Brittany than in Normandy, and these back-up plans would only have been actuated if the Normandy front had become a stalemate. In the event, the Operation *Cobra* break-out in late July 1944 put the Breton ports within reach once again.

GERMAN PLANS

German plans for Brittany were entirely reactive due to the crisis on the Normandy front. The steady attrition of German forces in Normandy forced Berlin to shift more and more of the divisions from Brittany into Normandy. Nevertheless, there was still concern that the Allies would conduct a second amphibious operation after D-Day. Although German planning expected that the Pas de Calais was the most likely alternative site, Brittany was also considered a high probability due to its extensive port facilities. As a result, 7. Armee was expressly forbidden from transferring any troops directly associated with coast defense from Brittany to Normandy such as naval and army coast artillery battalions. The Wehrmacht desperately tried to maintain four infantry divisions in Brittany, the minimum considered necessary to defend the coast. Although four divisions did remain in Brittany at the beginning of August, they had been so badly weakened that they offered little resistance to the American advance.

THE CAMPAIGN

THE PARTISAN WAR

The French resistance movement had a much greater impact in Brittany during the 1944 campaign than in most other regions. This was due to the unique conditions in the region along with a very active Allied special operations effort. Partisan activity was most intense in the western region of Brittany, an isolated rural area with extensive forests. This region retained its own distinct Celtic language and culture. Resentment against the German occupation intensified in 1943 due to agricultural requisitions which increased six-fold from 1941 to 1943. The German STO law (Service de Travail Obligatoire: forced labor) in 1943 swelled the ranks of the Maquis with young men fleeing this despised new imposition. The STO requisitions were increased in November 1943 to cover the age groups from 18 to 55. The main problem facing the Breton Maquis, until the summer of 1944, was the lack of weapons.

German anti-partisan operations in Brittany were conducted both by police and military organizations. The Gestapo in Brittany was directed by the Kommandeur der Sichereitspolizei und des SD under Obersturmbannführer Hartmut Pulmer, based in Rennes. This force was primarily involved in investigative and police work, and coordinated with the collaborationist French Milice. The German army's military police force, the Stadt and Orts Kommandantturen, operated Feldgendarmerie companies in most major towns. There were also larger formations in the major cities, including battalions from the Sicherungs-Regiment 56 in western Brittany and Sicherungs-Regiment 195 in eastern Brittany. As French resistance actions increased in the autumn of 1943, the Wehrmacht responded by deploying dedicated anti-partisan formations, often based on *Ost* battalions brought in from operations on the Russian Front. Although the *Osttruppen* were not trusted by the infantry division commanders, they were considered reliable for anti-partisan work. Russische-Bataillon 635 was a fairly typical example and consisted of 76 German officers and NCOs, 12 Russian officers and 515 Russian troops. These anti-partisan units were usually motorized, with this battalion having 186 vehicles and trucks. The *Osttruppen* were despised by the French for their brutality.

One of the army figures most closely associated with this effort was Gen.Maj. Christoph Graf zu Stolberg-Stolberg who led a variety of special purpose commands that employed *Osttruppen*. Stolberg was the commander for *Osttruppen* in the 7. Armee in Normandy and Brittany since November 1943. In April 1944, he was appointed to lead Divisionsstab z.b.V. 136 (zur besonderen Verwendung: Special Purpose Division Staff 136), formed from the previous z.b.V. 721. This anti-partisan force included two German infantry battalions from the 266. and 346. Infanterie Divisionen, Sicherungs-Bataillon 521, and four *Osttruppen* battalions: Ost-Bataillon 602 "Dnjepr", Russ.-Btl. 635, Wolga-Tatar-Btl. 627 and Ost-Reiter-Abt. 281; the last unit was a horse-cavalry battalion. The division had its own artillery component with two batteries of war-booty French 155mm guns. In August 1944, most of the *Osttruppen* units were transferred to the infantry divisions due to a shortage of manpower.

Regular infantry divisions sometimes participated in anti-partisan sweeps. Although Ramcke denied that the 2. Fallschirmjäger-Division participated in these actions, French accounts frequently identified involvement of "les parachutistes de Kreta" in reprisal actions due to their distinctive uniforms and armbands.

The British SOE maintained contacts in the region throughout the war but did not begin to deliver large quantities of arms until 1944. The BCRA developed a range of plans for the Maquis, the most significant of which was Plan *Vert* (Green) which aimed to cripple German rail traffic. This coincided with SHAEF plans to interdict German reinforcement of the Normandy front by bombing key rail links. In addition, it minimized the risk of German reprisals against civilians since the railway sabotage could be conducted away from towns and villages. Plan *Vert* was especially important in Brittany since most of the German divisions lacked sufficient transport and so relied on rail transport for long-distance transfers.

SHAEF opposed starting a national insurrection, Plan *Vidal*, until the last moment on the assumption that it would lead to massive German reprisals. Generalfeldmarschall Hugo Sperrle, deputy commander of OB West, issued a directive on February 3, 1944 that partisans involved in guerilla warfare were not to be taken prisoner; an OKW directive reaffirmed this on March 4, 1944. The level of violence in the Breton countryside continued to increase prior to D-Day, with no quarter given by either side.

The first large-scale Allied support for the Breton Maquis started in June 1944 with the dispatch of the troops of 4 SAS. These teams set up special camps in remote regions of Brittany to serve as rallying points for the Maquisards. The camps had radio transmitters for communications with London to coordinate the air delivery of weapons and equipment. The SAS also dispatched Cooney Parties to Brittany, small teams specializing in disrupting German railway traffic by demolishing tracks and bridges. The other special forces sent by air into Brittany were the Jedburgh teams. These were inter-Allied special operations teams intended to serve as liaison between the Maquisards and the regular Allied military formations.

By mid-June, the SAS teams at Camp Dingson in the Morbihan region near Malestroit had armed about 5,000 Maquisards, attracting German attention. The Germans staged a surprise attack on the camp on June 18, leading to a substantial firefight before the Germans finally forced the Maquisards to abandon the camp and scatter. The local Maquisards claimed that the fighting cost the Germans about 500 dead versus 200 Breton casualties. Other camps were organized, and additional Jedburgh teams parachuted into Brittany through the summer. By way of example, in the Côtes-du-Nord region of northern Brittany from July 10 to August 4, the local Maquisards claimed to have inflicted 2,500 German casualties, conducted 200 railway sabotage actions, derailed 40 trains, cut 200 telephone lines, conducted 50 ambushes, and captured 200 German trucks.

By July, SHAEF allocated 35 sorties per night to arm and equip the Maquisards in Brittany. Some 3,362 tons of supplies were airdropped to the Jedburgh teams in July 1944 alone. As guns and ammunition began flowing, one of the main problems for the Jedburgh teams was to restrain the Maquisards from premature armed action. Although ambushes, train derailments, and other mayhem was encouraged, the Allied leadership wanted the Breton Maquisards to refrain from full-scale partisan warfare until the arrival of the main Allied military formations. The final message to activate the Breton Maquisards came on the night of August 2, when the BBC broadcast the signal "Le chapeau de Napoleon est-il toujours à Perros-Guirec" (Napolean's cap is always in Perros-Guirec). By early August, there were about 35,000 armed Maquisards in Brittany and they controlled most of the rural areas.

The Jedburgh teams served as the connection between the Breton Maquis and the US Army. Major John W. Summers, codename Wyoming, was the leader of Jedburgh Team Horace that parachuted into the Brest area on the night of July 17–18. The team assisted the 6th Armored Division starting on August 8. Summers remained in the area and coordinated actions between the FFI and the 2nd Rangers during the fighting in the Le Conquet area later in the month. He was subsequently awarded the Distinguished Service Cross and Bronze Star.

It became increasingly dangerous for Germans to travel outside the main cities and garrisons. A report from Jedburgh Team Frederick described their experiences with the Maquisards in eastern Brittany:

> We found that for the most part the men we had to deal with were very brave, inclined to be far too rash, very fond of petty shootings which brought the whole weight of the Boche down on them, and very good comrades in a scrap. They show very little pity for the Boche with ample reason and none at all for the Milice whom they consider 100 per cent worse than the Boche. I personally witnessed the ill treatment and execution of five Milice and none of us felt the least pity for them. The fighting morale of the Maquis is really good. Volunteers were never lacking for the most dangerous missions and their one idea is to kill Boche. There is excellent material for the future army of France in their ranks.

Aside from the significant role played by the Breton Maquisards in the railway campaign in June–July 1944, their most important tactical role was in facilitating the rapid advance of the US Army's VIII Corps in August 1944, by securing key roads and bridges and preventing their destruction by German forces. Due to the weakness of the Wehrmacht in much of rural Brittany, the Maquisards controlled large areas of the Breton countryside by August 1944, and their units became strong enough to stand up to German infantry forces in many instances.

THE AMERICAN ADVANCE ON BRITTANY

The advance of Middleton's VIII Corps from Normandy into Brittany was accelerated by the collapse of the German defenses on the western flank of Choltitz's 84. Armee Korps in the wake of the Operation *Cobra* breakthrough. There were only two infantry divisions along the coast near

A column of M4 medium tanks of the 3rd platoon, Co. B, 8th Tank Battalion, 4th Armored Division advances through the wreckage of a German column in the Avranches area on their way into Brittany on July 31.

Advance into Brittany, August 1–12, 1944

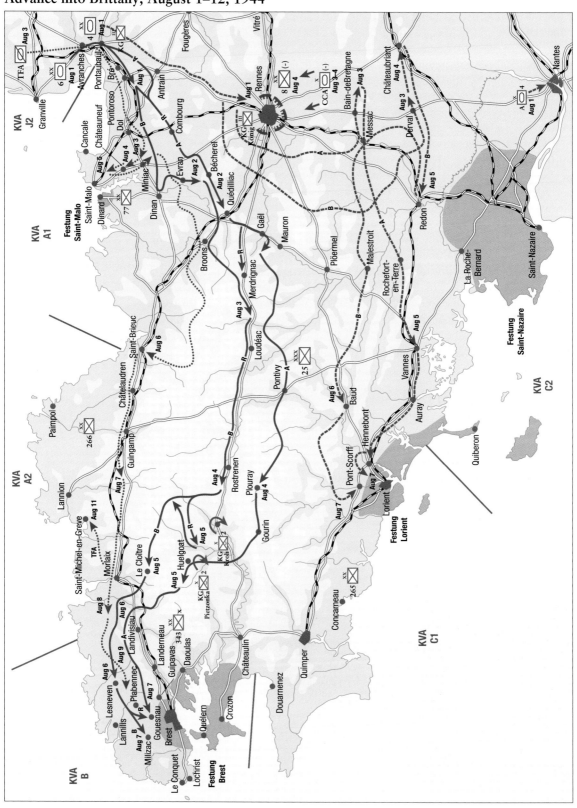

Coutances. The 243. Infanterie-Division was stationed from the coast to the eastern side of the Lessay–Avranches road. At the start of Operation *Cobra* on July 25, this division was extremely weak with only five battalions: one strong, two average, and two weak. The remnants of this division were expected to hold the key town of Coutances. Its neighbor to the east of the Lessay–Avranches road was the 91. Luftlande-Division, which only had two cadre battalions from its original formation, plus six other battalions amalgamated from shattered divisions. The six battalions consisted of two of average strength, one weak, and three exhausted. Both divisions took significant losses in the fighting with the 79th and 90th Infantry Divisions during the opening phase of Operation *Cobra*. The port of Granville south of Coutances had a substantial naval presence and numerous fortified coastal defense strongpoints. However, there was no substantial infantry presence in Granville beyond an *Ost* battalion.

The disintegration of the German defenses was accelerated by the growing chaos in the 7. Armee resulting from the Operation *Cobra* breakthrough. At 1900hrs on July 28, the 7. Armee commander, Gen. Paul Hausser ordered the 84. Armee Korps to withdraw to the southeast to escape American encirclement. The western flank on the coast, including the 91. Luftlande-Division and 243. Infanterie-Division, were expected to continue to withdraw southward. This created a gap between the weak western flank of 84. Armee Korps and the bulk of Choltitz's forces further east. Hausser's orders had been dispatched without the approval of the OB West commander, GFM Gunther Kluge. When he learned of Hausser's orders, "Kluge became almost violent." Kluge clearly understood that Hausser's orders had essentially opened the door to Middleton's VIII Corps to push its forces down along the coast, deep behind 7. Armee. Kluge sent countermanding orders, though few divisions received them. In the meantime, he attempted to activate a counter-attack force of the remaining Panzer force around Percy to close the Coutances–Avranches highway. In reality, this was impossible in the available time and under the chaotic conditions. Kluge sacked the 7. Armee chief-of-staff and probably would have done the same to Hausser except that his Waffen-SS connections made this politically impossible.

Following the 4th Armored Division through Avranches was the 8th Infantry Division. This is a company of the 28th Infantry marching past an abandoned 88mm Flak gun in Avranches on July 31, 1944.

The 15th-century stone bridge over the Sélune River at Pontaubault was the vital link between Normandy and Brittany. Unable to recapture it by ground attack, the bridge was subjected to nearly a week of air attacks by the Luftwaffe without success.

The 243. Infanterie Division was largely destroyed during this withdrawal, and its commander, Oberst Klosterkemper, arrived at the headquarters of 91. Luftlande Division on 30 July to warn them that his division no longer existed. The Kriegsmarine in Granville began demolishing the docks and other major installations starting on July 28, and shipped remaining equipment and personnel to Saint-Malo. Some of the naval personnel departed on coastal vessels, but most personnel had to leave by road and got caught up in the disorganized evacuation through Avranches. About three-quarters of the Granville garrison never reached Saint-Malo.

On July 28, Bradley ordered Middleton to commit the 4th and 6th Armored Divisions through his two forward infantry divisions to exploit the disintegration of the German defenses. Their mission was to push from Coutances south to Avranches and seize the bridges leading from Normandy into Brittany. The main source of delays for the two armored divisions was the congestion on the roads from the VIII Corps infantry divisions, and the mine threat. German resistance was extremely patchy, with occasional rearguard actions. By the end of the 28th, VIII Corps had control of Coutances, placing the armored divisions about 30 miles from Avranches.

On July 29, the 6th Armored Division stalled due to its caution in crossing the Sienne River, while Combat Command B of the 4th Armored Division advanced about ten miles. The superior performance of the 4th Armored Division led Middleton to order the division to take the lead in the liberation of Avranches. By this stage, the German defense consisted of small rearguards of the 91. Luftlande-Division. The advance of CCB, 4th Armored Division on July 30 nearly overran Hausser's advance command post, but Hausser and his staff escaped on foot. By the end of the day, the American columns had secured the two main highway bridges north of Avranches and a small force had advanced to the edge of the city. In the early morning hours, Middleton directed Brig. Gen. Holmes Dager, leading CCB 4th Armored Division, to take command of both CCB and CCA as well as an infantry regiment from the 8th Infantry Division. His mission was to complete the capture of Avranches, push on to the Sélune River bridges at Pontaubault, and secure the bridges leading into Brittany.

The situation in Avranches on the morning of July 31 was chaotic. Retreating German columns including the Granville garrison were trying to escape through the Avranches bottle-neck southward. They staged two improvised attacks against CCB 4th Armored Division during the morning to try to keep escape routes open; they were quickly overwhelmed. While CCB was clearing out Avranches, Brig. Gen. Bruce Clarke's CCA 4th Armored Division dispatched four task forces to the objectives further south.

Oberbefehlshaber West commander Kluge was shocked to discover that the Americans had reached Avranches so quickly. Realizing the importance of the Pontaubault bridges, he first tried to route two infantry divisions to the sector but quickly appreciated they would not arrive in time. Instead, he ordered Gen. der Art. Wilhelm Fahrmbacher, commanding 25. Armee Korps in neighboring Brittany, to strip the defenses of Saint-Malo and send them to gain control of the Sélune River bridges. All Fahrmbacher could scrape together was a battalion-strength *Kampfgruppe* under Oberst Rudolf Bacherer of the 77. Infanterie-Division. To reinforce Bacherer, Regiment-Gruppe Jäger was created further east consisting of 14 StuG III assault guns of I./Stug.Brig. 341, two battalions from Fallschirmjäger Ersatz und Ausbildungs Regiment 2, and one battalion from the 266. Infanterie-Division. The 2. Fallschirmjäger-Division created a *Kampfgruppe* called Fallschirmjäger-Regiment z.b.V. Rochlewski. This was led by a divisional staff officer, Oberstleutnant Rochlewski, and included III./FJR 7, an artillery battery from FS-Art. 2 and two infantry battalions from 25. Armee Korps with hearing and stomach problems. The assault guns attracted the attention of Allied fighter bombers and most were lost to air attack on July 31. By the time that the *Kampfgruppen* arrived near the bridges in the afternoon, CCA 4th Armored Division had already captured them. These units subsequently conducted a delaying action along the approaches to Saint-Malo.

When contacted by Berlin, Kluge described the situation as a "Riesensauerei:" a complete mess. Kluge blamed Hausser for his ill-advised decision to break-out to the south-east. In response to frantic phone calls from Berlin about the situation, he sarcastically suggested that the high command must be "living on the moon." He warned that "if the Americans get through at Avranches they will be out of the woods and they'll be able to do what they want.... The terrible thing is that there is not much that anyone could do.... It's a crazy situation."

When word arrived the Kampfgruppe Bacherer had failed to reach the bridges in time, Hitler ordered the Luftwaffe to attack the bridges. Due to Allied air superiority, the attacks had to be conducted at night. Dornier Do-217s of III./KG 100, based near Toulouse, began attacks on the night of August 2 using Hs 293 guided missiles. Attacks through to August 9 were ineffective, and nine aircraft were lost to Mosquito night-fighters and anti-aircraft fire. None of the guided missiles struck the bridge, though there was one near-miss.

Kluge asked Hitler for permission to redeploy the 2. Fallschirmjäger-Division from Brest and the 319. Infanterie-Division from the Channel Islands to set up defenses in front of Middleton. Hitler permitted the dispatch of the paratroopers, but would not tolerate any weakening of the Channel Islands, fearing that Britain planned to invade these prizes at any moment.

When the German counter-attacks failed to re-capture the bridges around Pontaubault, Hitler ordered the Luftwaffe to destroy them. The II./Kampfgeschwader 100 based in Toulouse began night attacks on the bridges using radio-guided Henschel Hs.293 guided air-to-surface missiles starting on the night of August 2/3, 1944 as shown in this illustration. The attacks were costly and failed to down any of the bridges.

By the morning of August 1, the 4th Armored Division had secured three bridges over the Sée River near Avranches and four over the Sélune River around Pontaubault. On this date, Patton's Third US Army was formally activated and Patton took over command of Middleton's VIII Corps. Since it appeared that German forces in the area were disintegrating, Patton ordered 4th Armored Division to race southward to Rennes, the Breton capital and main industrial city, to cut off the peninsula. The 6th Armored Division was to swing westward and head for the main objective, the port of Brest.

THE RACE FOR QUIBERON BAY

The 4th Armored Division advanced 40 miles in a single day, reaching the northern outskirts of Rennes by the evening of August 1. The divisional spearhead, Clarke's CCA, was repulsed by Flak Batterie Schmidt (2./gem. Flak Abt. 441(o)). This battery defended the Rennes airport and was armed with six 88mm FlaK guns and two 20mm quad automatic cannon. The airfield was struck by a sortie of 30 P-47 fighter bombers as well as divisional artillery. During the day, two replacement battalions reached Rennes from Le Mans to reinforce the Rennes garrison. They were put under the command of under Oberst Eugen König who had commanded the 91. Luftlande-Division before its destruction over the past few days. Some of these troops were used to reinforce the airfield battery. In the late evening, CCA attacked the airfield again but, after a two-hour battle, was unable to overcome the strongpoint. Eleven tanks were lost in the fighting.

By the morning of August 2, Maj. Gen. John Wood had decided that Rennes was too strongly garrisoned to capture it on the run. In discussions with Middleton, they agreed that this would be left for the 8th Infantry Division that was following behind. Instead, 4th Armored Division would continue to head south, swinging around the western side of Rennes. By August 3, this put the division's spearheads at Bain-le-Bretagne (CCA) and Derval (CCB). Middleton became anxious over the threat posed by the Rennes garrison to the 4th Armored Division's tail and, after reconsideration, insisted that Wood secure Rennes before proceeding any further. By the afternoon of August 3, the 13th Infantry, 8th Infantry Division was in position to attack into the northern suburbs of Rennes while Wood had returned part of CCA to the southern edge of the city late in the day. At 2300hrs, 7. Armee authorized the Rennes garrison commander, Oberstleutnant Barthel, to withdraw and this process began under the cover of darkness in the early morning hours. Two march columns set out for Saint-Nazaire to the south, largely avoiding US forces by staying away from the main roads. Although the 4th Armored Division had penetrated almost 20 miles south of Rennes, it was thinly stretched across the area. On August 4, the 13th Infantry Regiment, 8th Infantry Division marched into Rennes, followed by the remainder of the division later in the day.

Communication between Middleton's headquarters and Wood's forward headquarters was sporadic and on the afternoon of August 4, Middleton drove to meet Wood and clarify the division's mission. Wood had been arguing for several days that the division was better suited to a pursuit eastward toward Angers than to a siege operation south against the large ports of Lorient and Saint-Nazaire around Quiberon Bay. He had already sent CCB

This M18 76mm GMC was commanded by Sgt. Roger Turcan of Co. A, 704th Tank Destroyer Battalion, 4th Armored Division. While advancing on the airfield north of Rennes in August 1944, Turcan's vehicle was hit by a German anti-aircraft gun no fewer than seven times, killing three of the crew. Turcan remained with the vehicle, loading and firing the gun until he ran out of ammunition. He was later decorated with the Silver Star for his bravery.

east to Châteaubriant. Middleton was not clear on Patton's intentions, and so he instructed Wood to advance to Vannes and Lorient to cut off the base of the Breton Peninsula. Combat Command A reached Vannes on August 5 and found the town weakly protected, while CCB reached Lorient on August 7 and found that the defenses were substantial.

In fact, the defenses of Lorient were in a state of flux. The 25. Armee Korps headquarters under Gen. Wilhelm Fahrmbacher had reached the port on the evening of August 3. Lorient had been declared a "*Festung*" by Hitler, meaning that it would be defended to the last man. Defense of the port was oriented primarily seaward since Lorient had become a major Kriegsmarine operational base with submarine pens and other facilities. It originally had been under the protection of the 265. Infanterie-Division, but as troops were shifted from Brittany to Normandy earlier in the summer, the division also took responsibility of Saint-Nazaire. The focus of the division's defenses shifted to Lorient. The garrison in Lorient was substantial with more than 25,000 personnel, but this consisted mostly of Kriegsmarine forces associated with the port. The Festung Kommandant, Oberst Karl Kaumann, had no significant force at his disposal since most of the army troops were assigned to various artillery batteries or strongpoints. An improvised defense force was deployed in early August since the garrison possessed numerous artillery and Flak guns.

Dager's CCB reached Lorient on the morning of August 7 and started probing the city's defenses. After discovering an area near Pont Scorff that seemed to be weakly defended, a column was sent forward. This probe was greeted with heavy artillery fire that caused 105 casualties and destroyed five half-tracks, two armored cars, and numerous vehicles. Clarke's CCA arrived as well, but kept at arm's length from the port, which seemed to be bristling with guns. Attempts to scout the defenses using the division's artillery spotter aircraft found that the Flak was too dense to do so. Divisional intelligence estimated the garrison to have about 500 artillery pieces though the actual total was 197 guns, mainly in the coastal defense batteries, and 80 anti-tank guns. Major-General Wood sent a message to Middleton: "This is a job for infantry and guns. We should be allowed to reassemble and ready to hit again in a more profitable direction, namely to Paris. Believe infantry division should be sent here for this job."

Patton's Third US Army was still assigned the task of clearing the Breton ports, even if Middleton's VIII Corps did not have enough force to do so quickly. Middleton instructed Wood to contain Lorient until further decisions were made. Patton had instructed Middleton to send some troops to contain the port of Nantes, and Wood dispatched all of Clarke's CCA. Although the Nantes mission might have seemed a minor operation, it lay at the mouth of the Loire River and so could provide a staging area for an eventual push eastward to Paris. On the afternoon of August 12, CCA and local French resistance groups liberated the city. A day later, Wood got his wish and the 4th Armored Division was ordered out of Brittany to take part in the race for Paris.

THE RACE TO BREST

While the 4th Armored Division was heading south towards Quiberon Bay, Maj. Gen. Robert Grow's 6th Armored Division was heading west towards the port of Brest. Patton had visited the divisional command post on August 1 and told them that he had wagered a bet with Montgomery that US troops would be in Brest by Saturday, August 5 – 200 miles in five days. Patton's instructions were to bypass resistance. Grow's first challenge was to move the division through the bottleneck of the old Pontaubault Bridge over the Sélune River. Grow's plan was to move in two columns, CCA in the north and CCB and CCR (Reserve) south. Although there was some German resistance near the start line along the Cousnon River, once CCR began rolling, it encountered very little resistance. German activity seemed far worse behind them than in front. Avranches had become a focus of German attention, with repeated Luftwaffe attacks, including the night missile attacks mentioned earlier. German strongpoints were encountered sporadically, such as a battalion-sized force at a crossroads near Mauron on August 3.

The advance was greatly facilitated by the French resistance, which was especially active in Brittany. Aside from direct contact between the 6th Armored Division and elements of the FFI, the widespread activities of the French insurgents discouraged the Germans from deploying small rearguard units to block the American advance since these actions usually attracted violent French attention.

The advance was temporarily halted late on August 3 when Middleton sent instructions that 6th Armored Division should divert north to assist Task Force A and the 83rd Division liberate the port of Saint-Malo. The divisions spent the morning of August 4 reconfiguring for the change of plans when Patton unexpectedly showed up at Grow's command post. Patton was infuriated that Grow had halted and asked him on whose authority he had done so. After being handed Middleton's order by Grow, Patton replied: "You go ahead where I told you to go. I'll see Middleton." To make up the day's delay, Grow ordered a night march, assuming that there would be little or no opposition, thanks in no small measure to FFI help.

By the later part of the week, communications between Middleton's VIII Corps and the 6th Armored Division had largely vanished due to the distances involved. Grow wanted Middleton to push supplies and military police behind him to deal with growing supply problems.

One of the few German units active to the east of Brest was the 2. Fallschirmjäger-Division, stationed near Brest. On August 3, the division was ordered to move towards Normandy to take part in counter-attacks against the Pontaubault bridgehead. As mentioned earlier, the division had already shed one of its battalions to form a *Kampfgruppe* in the initial attacks on the bridge. Much of the remainder of the division set off in two columns. Kampfgruppe Pietzonka was the northern column and consisted of Fallschirmjäger-Regiment 7, reinforced with I./Grenadier-Regiment 851 from the neighboring 343. Infanterie-Division, two anti-tank companies, and an artillery detachment. South of this was Kampfgruppe Kroh, consisting of Fallschirmjäger-Regiment 2, along with the divisional Pionier and tank destroyer units. The division first came in contact with Allied forces on August 4 when a reconnaissance detachment under Oberleutnant Jahn ahead of the main body was wiped out near Rostrenen, apparently by an FTP unit associated with Jedburgh Team Frederick. As it became obvious that the main body of the division would be unable to reach Normandy in time, the two *Kampfgruppen* were told to halt and take up defensive positions on the approaches to Brest.

French resistance units monitored the progress of the German paratroopers and warned CCB of the concentration of Kampfgruppe Kroh around Carhaix on August 5, prompting the American unit to skirt around the town. In the meantime, CCA encountered Kampfgruppe Pietzonka in Huelgoat, about 40 miles from Brest. This led to a firefight lasting several hours, in the wooded and rough hill country nearby. The fighting eventually enveloped Kampfgruppe Kroh, which encountered US and French resistance

A column of M4 medium tanks of Co. B, 69th Tank Battalion, 6th Armored Division advances towards Brest in August 1944.

An M5A1 light tank of the 6th Armored Division passes through Rostrenen on August 4 on its way to Brest. The town square is guarded by a detachment of Maquisards and a US military policeman. Combat Command B led the way through the town that day, followed by CCR.

forces. Combat Command A eventually broke contact since Clarke did not want to waste time dealing with the German paratroopers ensconced in the dense woods nearby. The reduction of the German defenses were left to the local FFI Maquis and bitter fighting continued for a few days.

The fighting around Huelgoat had a curious turn a week later. About 130 paratroopers were captured by the Maquis and held in the town of Brasprats, east of Brest. One German paratrooper escaped and made it back to the 2. Fallschirmjäger-Division headquarters. Ramcke suspected the prisoners would be executed by the French. Leutnant Erich Lepkowski, commander of 5./FJR 2, volunteered to lead a small group of paratroopers from his company to rescue them using some captured American vehicles. The situation in the rural areas was still fluid at the time, and the American vehicles were unlikely to attract the attention of the local Maquis. On August

In mid-August, the 6th Armored Division was relieved of its responsibilities in the Brest area and sent instead to take over the containment of Festung Lorient from the 4th Armored Division. Here, a group of officers of one of the division's armored infantry battalions discuss the move on August 17.

16, Lepkowski and his men reached Brasparts, freed the prisoners and drove them back to German lines. Ramcke later recommended him for the Oak Leaves of the Knight's Cross for his leadership on this raid.

Combat Command B reached the northern outskirts of Brest on August 6 with the remainder of the division arriving on the 7th. Grow believed that the city might be weakly held and might surrender. However, scouts began to report that there were formidable defenses around the outskirts of the city. Grow sent a surrender ultimatum to the German garrison, but it was refused. Plans were formulated to start an assault on August 8. Before this occurred, the rear areas of the division began to erupt in small-scale fighting with scattered German units. Later in the day, the 212th Armored Field Artillery Battalion captured a German divisional headquarters staff led by Gen.Lt. Karl Spang. He was the commander of the 266. Infanterie-Division. His division had shed several of its battalions to assist in the defense of Dinan and Saint-Malo, and the rest of the division had been ordered to reinforce the Brest garrison. Spang was completely unaware of the presence of the 6th Armored Division, and so various march groups collided with American troops in a completely uncoordinated fashion. By this time, the 266. Infanterie-Division was only about a regiment in size. By the morning of August 9, there were numerous fire-fights around the divisional perimeter. About a thousand German troops were captured that day by CCR, about half the division, while the rest infiltrated into Brest.

The objectives of the 6th Armored Division changed abruptly due to a significant amendment to the *Overlord* plan. The rout of the 7. Armee and the collapse of its left wing in early August led Wood and Patton to begin to question the role to be played by Third US Army. On August 3, Bradley changed the mandate to the use of a "minimum of forces" for the Brittany mission, namely Middleton's VIII Corps. The Cherbourg campaign suggested that even if the Breton ports were secured quickly, it would take months for them to begin to provide supplies due to likely German demolition efforts. When German resistance emerged at Saint-Nazaire and Brest, the question was raised whether to use other corps of the Third US Army to lay siege to the ports, or whether it would not be more profitable to send these corps eastward in the hopes that other ports further east on the Channel such as Le Havre and Boulogne could be secured. By the end of the first week of August, a consensus was emerging between Bradley, Montgomery, and Eisenhower that the Brittany mission should take a back seat to the race for the Seine. This became manifest when the 4th Armored Division was ordered to re-orient eastward into the Loire Valley on August 12–13. At the same time, Grow's 6th Armored Division was ordered to return eastward to Lorient and Vannes to take the place of the 4th Armored Division while leaving only CCA and a battalion from the 8th Infantry Division to contain Brest until a siege force could be sent there later in the month. The newly arrived Ninth US Army would be given the Brittany mission later in August.

THE RACE ALONG THE NORTHERN COAST

At the beginning of August, Middleton's VIII Corps had four divisions, the 4th and 6th Armored Divisions and the 8th and 83rd Infantry Divisions. The two armored divisions were immediately committed to the race for the ports, and 8th Infantry Division was instructed to follow behind 4th Armored Division to cut off the Breton Peninsula. This left 83rd Infantry Division following behind the rest of the corps. Patton recognized that this division was not suitable for fast pursuit, so he had Middleton create Task Force A to conduct a pursuit along the northern Breton coast in parallel to the 6th Armored Division further south. Task Force A, commanded by Brig. Gen. Herbert Earnest, was based around the headquarters staff of the 6th Tank Destroyer Group and its main elements were the 15th Cavalry Group and 159th Engineer Battalion. It was roughly a regiment in size, numbering about 3,500 troops. The Task Force A mission was to secure the major bridges along the route Dol-de-Bretagne–Dinan–Guingamp. Except for the bridges, the task force was instructed to bypass any resistance. There was considerable hope that the FFI resistance groups would facilitate the mission.

Task Force A encountered difficulties on entering Brittany on August 3, running into Kampfgruppe Bacherer and a few StuG III assault guns of StuG.Brig. 341. Earnest decided to skirt around these defenses. The mission orders were changed almost immediately, as Middleton was concerned that the accumulation of German forces around the port of Saint-Malo might threaten the advance of the 6th Armored Division. Earnest was ordered to probe towards Saint-Malo, and quickly ran into significant German defenses on the approaches to Châteauneuf-d'Ille-et-Villane. After requesting infantry reinforcement, Middleton directed the 330th Infantry of the 83rd Infantry Division to meet up with Task Force A and attempt a quick capture of Saint-Malo. Actions around the periphery of Saint-Malo on August 4–5 made it clear that the garrison was larger than anticipated and would defend the port. Patton was unwilling to divert the 6th Armored Division to this mission, so Middleton was forced to wait until the 83rd Infantry Division could be brought forward to begin the main attack. The diversion to Saint-Malo delayed Task Force A for nearly two days from its westbound mission until late on August 5.

Task Force A eventually assisted the Maquis in the Côte du Nord area to deal with several German strongpoints along the coast. Among these was HKB 1272 in strongpoint Po27 near Plounez. This army battery was armed with two 203mm K(E) SKC/34 railway guns in a concrete kettle position on a turntable. The site had been heavily bombed, and it was abandoned before the arrival of Task Force A when the 266. Infanterie-Division withdrew from the area into Festung Brest.

On August 4, the Special Forces detachment assigned to Third US Army contacted Jedburgh Team Felix who indicated that the FFI had secured all the northern bridges along the Task Force A route from Dinan through Guingamp and Morlaix. Before noon on August 6, Task Force A found that the FFI had already secured Brieuc and its key bridges. They met with Col. Albert Eon, head of the Inter-Allied mission that was setting up the EMFFI headquarters in Brittany to coordinate the FFI missions. Task Force A continued to advance westward with the assistance of the FFI and Jedburgh teams. When German resistance was encountered, the FFI teams circumvented the strongpoints to determine whether there was a substantial German force ahead or only a rearguard. As a result, the Task Force was able to move quickly all the way to Morlaix. This town contained a major bridge and it had been garrisoned by the 266. Infanterie-Division. However, on August 8, before the arrival of Task Force A, the 266. Infanterie-Division had departed for Brest as mentioned earlier. On the morning of 9 August, Task Force A took the last remaining bridge south of Morlaix, completing their mission. In total, Task Force A and the associated FFI detachments had captured about 1,500 German troops and had secured all the main bridges along the northern Breton coast.

Middleton planned to recall Task Force A back to the Saint-Malo area, but Col. Eon asked that it remain to assist the FFI in clearing the German strongpoint at Paimpol. This strongpoint was used to ferry supplies to the Channel Islands and the coastal batteries there could interfere with the Allies use of the port of Saint-Brieuc. Eon indicated that the FFI would provide about 2,500 Maquisards to conduct the main fighting, but that American motor transport and a few armored vehicles would be of considerable assistance. In the event, a four-day battle ensued starting with the German strongpoint at Lézardrieux on the approaches to Paimpol. This town had been the headquarters of a battalion of GR 897 (266. Infanterie–Division) and included a fortified battery of Artillerie-Regiment. 266. Much of this unit had already departed, but the town had ten fortified strongpoints and a rear guard force. After some fighting, the defenses were overcome and 430 prisoners taken. The Task Force A/FFI group next headed to Paimpol itself. This small port city was heavily fortified with numerous strongpoints. It had been the site of a fortified railroad gun battery, though the guns had been spiked during the withdrawal of 266. Infanterie-Division. The garrison there was overcome by noon on August 17 and 2,000 prisoners captured.

The rapid advance of Task Force A along the Côtes-du-Nord was one of the best examples of the effective interaction of the US Army and the FFI. While it is not apparent from US official accounts, much of the mission of Task Force A had already been accomplished by FFI detachments in the first week of August, with the US troops securing these liberated towns and villages. Due to the withdrawal of the 266. Infanterie-Division, fighting was very modest.

THE BATTLE OF SAINT-MALO

The *Festung* commander of Saint-Malo was Oberst Andreas von Aulock. The US Army estimated the German garrison in the Saint-Malo area to number 3,000 to 6,000 troops; the FFI estimated 10,000 troops. In reality,

A B-24J of the 565th Bomb Squadron, 389th Bomb Group takes part in the attack on Saint-Malo on August 13, 1944. Saint-Malo itself is covered in smoke while explosions rock Fort National. The peninsula above the bomber's tail is Pointe de la Varde, site of Fort de la Varde. This particular aircraft was destroyed a day later in a crash-landing at RAF Hethel.

the garrison in early August 1944 was about 12,000 troops, due to the arrival of troops retreating from the Granville and Avranches areas. The area had been heavily fortified as part of the Atlantic Wall program, amplifying existing French fortifications in the area. Although most of the fortifications were oriented seaward, there was a fortified *Landfront* on both sides of the Rance River. The town had originally been defended by the 77. Infanterie-Division but its main force had been sent to re-take the Ponaubault Bridge. After this mission had failed, the remnants of the division under Oberst Rudolf Bacherer, was ordered to return to the Saint-Malo sector. The III./GR 897 of the 266. Infanterie-Division was also directed to Saint-Malo after its failed mission at the Pontaubault Bridge. The other army troops stationed in the Saint-Malo area included three anti-partisan battalions: Ost-Bataillon 602 (Russ) Ost-Bataillon 635 (Russ) and Sicherungs-Bataillon 1220.

The Luftwaffe had a significant presence in Saint-Malo in the form of Flak-Regiment 15 and other air defense units. The Kriegsmarine operated out of the port under the command of Kapt. zur See Werner Endell who served as the Hafo Saint-Malo (*Hafenkommandant*: Harbor commander) and also as Aulock's second-in-command once the battle started.

There were also a number of coastal gun batteries in the area, under the direction of Marine-Artillerie-Abteilung 260 and Heeres-Küsten-Bataillon 1271.

Saint-Malo had been heavily fortified over the centuries due to its strategic location. These older French fortifications were substantially amplified by the Atlantic Wall program. The overall defense position was designated Küsten Verteidigung Gruppe Rance, named after the river Rance that ran to the sea at Saint-Malo. This group consisted of three sub-groups, KVU Dol covering the town of Dol-de-Bretagne east of Saint-Malo, KVU Cancale covering the peninsula northeast of Saint-Malo, and

Two of the army artillery batteries in the Saint-Malo area, in strongpoint Ra.155a in Dinard and strongpoint Ra.160a in Paramé, were armed with war-booty French Schneider 155mm howitzers, known as the 15.5cm sFH.414(f) in Wehrmacht service. Many were removed from the coastal emplacements and used during the fighting along the Landfront in August 1944.

KVU St-Malo, covering the city and the related towns around Saint-Malo. KVU St-Malo was the largest of the three, consisting of 79 fortified defense nests compared to 16 in KVU Cancale and only seven in KVU Dol. The city presented a complicated battlefield since the area was split in half by the Rance River.

Major-General Robert Macon's 83rd Infantry Division arrived at Dol-de-Bretagne on August 4 and began deploying its three regiments on the east side of the Rance River. On the western side, the 329th Infantry met up with Task Force A near Châteauneuf and advanced along the Rance River on August 5 before Task Force A departed for its mission westward. On the eastern side, the 331st Infantry advanced along the Bay of Mont Saint-Michel and crossed over the first line of anti-tank traps and obstacles near Saint-Benoît-des-Ondres. The city's civilian population was evacuated by order of the *Festung* commander, Oberst von Aulock, on the evening of August 5.

Serious fighting began on the afternoon of August 6 as the three regiments of the 83rd Infantry Division reached the outskirts of the fortified defenses. Middleton realized that additional forces would be necessary, and so diverted the 121st Infantry of the 8th Infantry Division from Rennes. He also added another field artillery battalion from corps reserve.

In the sector of the 330th Infantry on the outskirts of Saint-Malo, the main defensive hurdle was Kampfabschnitt Josefsberg, the German name for the agglomeration of strongpoints around Mont Saint-Joseph. This hill was formed of the solid granite bedrock and had strongpoints carved into the cliffs. The defenses included an army coastal battery with four war-booty French 155mm howitzers. It proved pointless to try to take the position with infantry, and so field artillery and tank destroyers were brought up to reduce the positions one-by-one. The German defenders surrendered on August 9 and there were about 400 survivors.

A squad from Company I, 331st Infantry advances along Rue de la Gardelle on August 8 during the fighting for the Paramé suburb.

Reduction of Saint-Malo, August 4–17, 1944

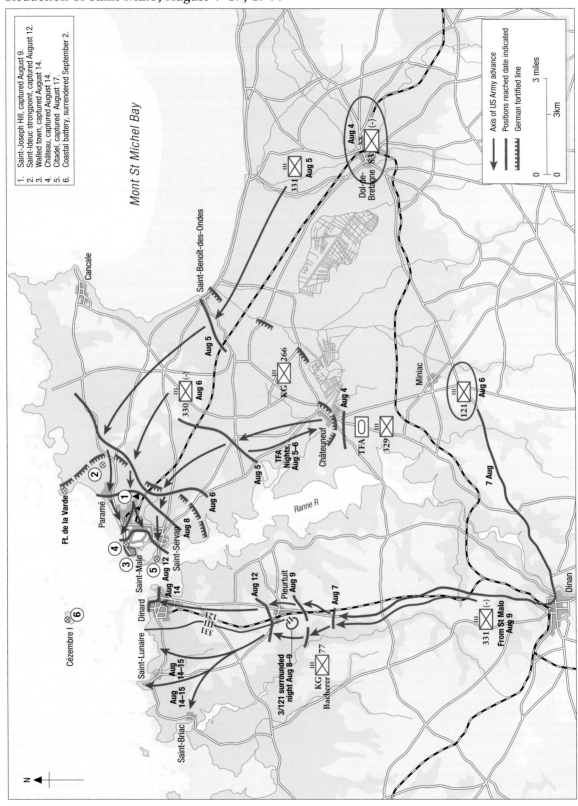

1. Saint-Joseph Hill, captured August 9.
2. Saint-Ideuc strongpoint, captured August 12.
3. Walled town, captured August 14.
4. Château, captured August 14.
5. Citadel, captured August 17.
6. Coastal battery, surrendered September 2.

Mont St Michel Bay

Cancale

Saint-Benoît-des-Ondes

Dol-de-
Bretagne

Aug 4

Aug 5

331
Aug 5

330
Aug 6

KG 266
Aug 5

Châteuneuf
Aug 4

TFA
Nights,
Aug 5–6

TFA

329

121
Aug 6

Miniac

7 Aug

Ranne R

Aug 5

Aug 6

Aug 8

Ft. de la Varde

Paramé

Saint-Servan

Saint-Malo

Aug 12

Aug 14

Cézembre I

Dinard

Saint-Lunaire

Saint-Briac

Aug
14–15

Aug
14–15

331
121

Aug 12

Pleurtuit
Aug 9

Aug 7

3/121 surrounded
night Aug 8–9

KG 77
Bacherer

331
From St Malo
Aug 9

Dinan

Legend:
Axis of US Army advance
Positions reached date indicated
German fortified line

0   3km
0   3 miles

N

On August 9, troops of the 331st Infantry escort away several German prisoners from the Reichenau-Kaserne, the former École de Police National, on Rue Hippolyte de la Morvonnais. The three German troops in the black uniforms in the center are Kreigsmarine troops.

The reduction of Kampfabschnitt Josefsberg proved to be central to the overall battle and its elimination allowed the regiments on either side to advance. The 329th Infantry pushed through Saint-Servan to the southern walls of Saint-Malo, and the 331st Infantry pushed through the Paramé suburb. By this stage, the 83rd Infantry Division had captured about 3,500 German troops, more than a quarter of the garrison.

The 121st Infantry was directed to the western side of the Rance River to deal with the Dinard garrison. This area was defended by the remnants of the 77. Infanterie-Division under Oberst Bacherer along with a few StuG

The Zitadelle was based on the 18th-century Fort de la Cité. It was located on the end of the small Aleth Peninsula and can be seen on the far left of this reconnaissance photo taken during the fighting; Saint-Servan-sur-Mer is to the right.

This is a view of the Zitadelle from the neighboring village of Saint-Servan-sur-Mer shortly after the impact of an aircraft bomb.

III from StuG-Brigade 341. Bacherer's force took advantage of the numerous fortifications in this sector to set up a series of effective strongpoints. On the afternoon of August 8, the 3/121st Infantry became isolated from the rest of the regiment when a few StuG III with accompanying infantry reoccupied a strongpoint previously cleared by the battalion. The slow progress of the 121st Infantry convinced Macon to pay more attention to the situation west of the Rance and he decided to reconfigure his forces. He transferred the 331st Infantry to assist the 121st Infantry on the west side of the river, leaving the other two regiments to deal with the final reduction of Saint-Malo. Nevertheless, progress towards Dinard was still slow, and the isolated 3/121st Infantry was not reached until the afternoon of August 12 when the defenses around Pleurtuit were overcome. The two regiments finally fought their way into Dinard on August 14. The city was cleared on August 15 along with the neighboring villages of Saint-Lunaire and Saint-Briac-sur-Mer. This added about 4,000 more prisoners.

The remaining defenses around Saint-Malo consisted of the walled town itself, the Zitadelle, and Fort de la Varde. The Zitadelle (Citadel) was the German name for the Fort de la Cité d'Aleth, located on a peninsula extending

An American flag flies above the Zitadelle, the Fort de la Cité d'Aleth, after the surrender on August 17. The R105 bunker was designed as a Flak position and these were used for 40mm Bofors guns operated by the 5./M.Fla.Abt. 806, a naval anti-aircraft battalion.

into the Rance estuary south of Saint-Malo. The 330th Infantry was assigned to take Fort de la Varde, located on a peninsula jutting out into the bay. In the foreground to the fort was the fortified neighborhood of Saint-Ideuc on the eastern side of Paramé. This area was subjected to artillery fire starting on August 9, and two battalions of the 330th Infantry with engineer support began to methodically attack the numerous pillboxes and strongpoints in Saint-Ideuc. This area was cleared by the late afternoon of August 12, with 160 survivors finally surrendering. The fort was attacked next and the garrison of about a hundred surrendered on the evening of August 13.

The remaining battalion of the 330th Infantry attacked the northeast corner of Saint-Malo including the casino and the fortified château. The casino was captured on August 11, but the château continued to resist. Artillery fire set many structures within Saint-Malo ablaze, and on the afternoon of August 13, a truce was declared to allow for the escape of about a thousand French civilians in Saint-Malo as well as another 500 hostages and internees kept in the old Fort National on an island immediately off the coast. On the morning of August 14, all three battalions of the 330th Infantry were assigned to task of reducing Saint-Malo. The town itself was not heavily defended due to the numerous fires. Nevertheless, it took a day of close-range fire against the château to convince the last 150 survivors to surrender. On August 16, a rifle company of the 329th Infantry waited until low tide to cross to Fort National and Grand Bey, netting a further 150 German prisoners.

This is a view from the top of the Zitadelle after the surrender looking to the north across the bay to Saint-Malo. Several of the bunkers in this sector were assigned to the harbor commander, Kapt.z.S. Werner Endell.

The last defenses in the harbor area were the Zitadelle and the fortified island of Cézembre. Before becoming Aulock's command post, the Zitadelle was called Stützpunkt 230 and was occupied by an army *Festung-Stamm-Kompanie*, as well as naval troops of the MAA 608 staff and 5./M.Fla.Abt. 806. Macon attempted to use artillery to reduce the

Zitadelle, and by this point some ten field artillery battalions were involved including 240mm howitzers. The main problem was a shortage of artillery ammunition. There were also numerous attempts to reduce the fortifications using air attack, but to little avail. The garrison in the Zitadelle, including Aulock himself, were bolstered by the news that Panzergruppe West in Normandy was launching a Panzer offensive towards Avranches that would cut off the US Army in Brittany and relieve the Saint-Malo garrison. On August 9, a rifle company of the 329th Infantry attempted to advance into the Zitadelle through gaps caused by the aerial attacks. This was repulsed by heavy fire. The Zitadelle was struck again by medium bombers on August 13 and August 15, along with a continual stream of fire from field artillery and tank destroyers. Finally, two massive 8in. guns of the corps artillery were brought to within 1,500 yards of the fortress to direct fire at portholes and vents. The 4.2in. mortars switched their mixture of ammunition to

include more incendiary white phosphorous rounds. A planned bombing attack using napalm was scheduled for August 17, but instead, Aulock sent out an emissary to arrange the surrender of the remaining 400 troops. This ended the fighting on the mainland, though the fortified island of Cézembre remained. By this stage, the 83rd Infantry Division had captured about 10,000 German troops.

Cézembre Island was 4,000 yards off shore and had been heavily fortified under the Atlantic Wall program. The island was commanded by Oberleutnant (Marine Artillerie) Richard Seuss and normally had a garrison of 241 men to man the battery there, 1./MAA 608. This was equipped with war-booty French 194mm guns as well as anti-aircraft guns and defensive weapons. The coastal guns on the island could interfere with maritime traffic into the ports of Saint-Malo, Granville, and Cancale. Air attacks against the island began on August 6, and the napalm attack intended for the Zitadelle on August 17 was directed against Cézembre instead. Offers were made to secure the garrison's surrender, but they were refused. There was some planning done for an amphibious assault, but instead, the artillery and air bombardment continued sporadically as resources were available. After another surrender offer was refused on September 1, the battleship HMS *Warspite* was brought up to pound the island with its 15in. guns. The 330th Infantry was slated to conduct an amphibious landing on September 2, but the garrison raised a white flag. The bombardment had finally managed to damage the water distillation plant, and 323 troops surrendered, including two Italian officers.

THE AVRANCHES COUNTER-ATTACK FAILS

After the weak counter-attack to re-capture the Pontaubault Bridge near Avranches had failed, the OB West commander, Gunter von Kluge, began to take steps to prepare a much larger counter-offensive. Hitler saw this an opportunity to counter the success of the Operation *Cobra* breakthrough in Normandy with the secondary benefit of cutting off Patton's Third US Army. This grandiose plan was codenamed *Lüttich* (Liege). The attack force consisted of the several Panzer divisions that had been resisting the British attacks south of Caen. They were pulled out of the line and replaced by infantry divisions in the first week of August. The objective was to push across the front of the First US Army to reach Avranches. The Panzer counter-offensive started around midnight on August 6–7 and first made contact with elements of the 30th Infantry Division around the town of Mortain. The Ultra signals intelligence system had learned of the plans hours before the attack, and the 30th Infantry Division was ordered to hunker down for an attack. The German units made only modest gains against the entrenched infantry, and clear skies that day permitted a massive wave of Allied fighter bomber attacks that paralyzed the German advance.

Operation *Lüttich*, the German Panzer counter-offensive to cut off the US Army at Avranches, was stopped almost immediately in a violent confrontation with the 30th Infantry Division in the hills around Mortain. This is a pair of Panther Ausf. A tanks and a SdKfz 251 half-track of 1. SS-Panzer-Division "Leibstandarte Adolf Hitler" knocked out in the fighting with the 117th Infantry Regiment near Saint-Barthélemy. This allowed VIII Corps to continue the Brittany operation without concern about its links to the rest of the Third US Army.

On the morning of August 8, the First Canadian Army launched Operation *Totalize*, an offensive aimed at Falaise, 21 miles south of Caen. For the Allies, the timing of Operation *Lüttich* could hardly have been better. The Germans had denuded the British sector of Panzer units precisely before the Canadian offensive. Kluge managed to halt the movement of the second wave of Panzer divisions so that they could return to resist the Canadian drive. A more ominous development was Patton's capture of Le Mans, which strongly hinted that the Allies were in the process of carrying out a deep envelopment of the German forces in Normandy.

Hitler insisted that the Mortain attack be resumed by August 11. However, by the evening of the 10th, the situation in Normandy was nearing a crisis. The Canadians had resumed their attack towards Falaise, and Patton's XV Corps had begun to swing to the northeast towards the main German supply center in Alençon. Kluge asked Berlin to call off Operation *Lüttich* to free up two or three Panzer divisions to counter-attack Patton's spearheads around Alençon. Operation *Lüttich* had accomplished nothing but to fatally weaken the German defenses in the Caen sector. The price for this mistake would be the encirclement at Falaise.

Operation *Lüttich* never proceeded far enough to threaten the operations of Middleton's VIII corps in Brittany, even though its ultimate objective had been to trap the American forces there by cutting them off at Avranches.

THE BATTLE FOR BREST: THE DAOULAS PENINSULA

The decision to re-orient the 6th Armored Division eastward to central France led to the temporary delay in the plans to assault Festung Brest. Middleton's shrinking VIII Corps simply did not have the resources to do much more than contain the port in early August. In mid-August, Bradley ordered the transfer of the 2nd and 29th Infantry Divisions to the Brest mission. The 8th Infantry Division was freed from its responsibilities in eastern Brittany in mid-August and moved to Brest. The 2nd Infantry Division arrived in the area around August 19 and the 29th Infantry Division on August 23. The main shortfall was in the ammunition supply, which was gradually increased to 8,000 tons – enough for about six-days of intense combat. In general, the US Army underestimated the size and tenacity of the German garrison in Brest.

While forces were massing for the main attack, Middleton decided to isolate Brest by securing both flanks. The first of the attacks was directed against the Armorique (Daoulas) Peninsula on the eastern side of the Bay of Brest. This peninsula had a number of hills with commanding views over Brest, and the coastal artillery batteries could fire on advancing American troops. Middleton directed the 2nd Infantry Division to create Task Force B, led by the division's assistant commander Brig. Gen. James Van Fleet, to carry out this mission.

Jedburgh Team Horace helped a company of ex-Soviet *Osttruppen* from Ost-Bataillon 633 under Capt. Rozumovich to defect to the Breton FFI on August 9 during the fighting near Plougastel. They were later assigned to aid Task Force Sugar in the fighting around Le Conquet. Here, Lt. Kitayev discusses plans to contain Stützpunkt Kerlouchan with an officer from the 2nd Rangers on August 28.

This force consisted mainly of the 38th Infantry Regiment, the 50th Armored Infantry from the 6th Armored Division and Task Force A.

The German forces on the peninsula originally were led by Oberst Förster, commander of Festung-Grenadier-Regiment 852. They consisted of two battalions from the division's FGR 851 and 852, survivors from 266. Infanterie-Division, Ost-Bataillon 633, and Kriegsmaine artillery and Flak units. In total, these forces numbered about 3,600 men. Ramcke was not happy about the defenses on the peninsula, characterizing the commander as "having an appreciation for good food and leisure, and not up to the job." He was replaced by Oberst Baumann, commander of Grenadier-Regiment 851. Ramcke also decided to stiffen the defense by adding three companies from III./ FJR 7 and a paratrooper anti-tank company.

The initial objective of Task Force B was Hill 154, locally called the "colline de Kerudu," a high point along the Etorn River that effectively blocked entrance to the peninsula. Due to its obvious importance, this hill had been reinforced during the Atlantic Wall program as strongpoint Br. 390. The principal force defending the area was III./GR 852 and Ost-

Btl. 633, both from 343. Infanterie-Division, reinforced with paratroopers. It contained a small naval Flak detachment from M.Fla.Abt. 811 with three Flak guns, along with eight bunkers, about two-dozen machine-gun nests and an extensive trench system. The hill had been cleared of foliage, giving the weapons a clear field of fire.

Task Force B began to advance from Landernau on August 21 and quickly reached Hill 154. Heavy machine-gun, mortar, and artillery fire halted the advance. Hill 154 posed a problem since it was a rocky outcropping with very little cover. Reinforced with tank destroyers and additional artillery support, the 38th Infantry assaulted the hill on August 23. During the action, Staff Sgt. Alvin Casey charged a pillbox that was blocking the advance, knocking it out with grenades. He was mortally wounded and posthumously awarded the Medal of Honor. A total of 143 German prisoners were taken in addition more than 100 dead around the hilltop. The 38th Infantry was later awarded the Presidential Unit Citation for its actions that day.

The capture of Hill 154 opened up access to the peninsula and prompted the Germans to demolish the nearby Albert-Louppe Bridge that connected the peninsula to Brest over the Etorn River. This effectively isolated the remainder of the German forces on the peninsula from the port. Over the course of the next week, Task Force B continued to push south to mop up the German defenses with 38th Infantry to the north and the 50th Armored Infantry to the south. By the end of August, Task Force B had captured 3,039 prisoners and had overrun two more naval 105mm Flak batteries, 4./M. Fla.Abt. 804 at Kerziou and 1./M.Fla.Abt. 811 at Kerdéniel, and the 40mm

Middleton's surrender ultimatum was answered by Ramcke on August 19–20 in a series of exchanges. Here, a blind-folded *Fallschirmjäger* officer delivers a set of messages to Maj. Gen. Donald Stroh, commander of the 8th Infantry Division, at his command post outside Brest. The exchanges included a request from Ramcke that the US avoid bombing or shelling the main Wehrmacht hospital facility inside Brest.

Defenses of Festung Brest, August 25, 1944

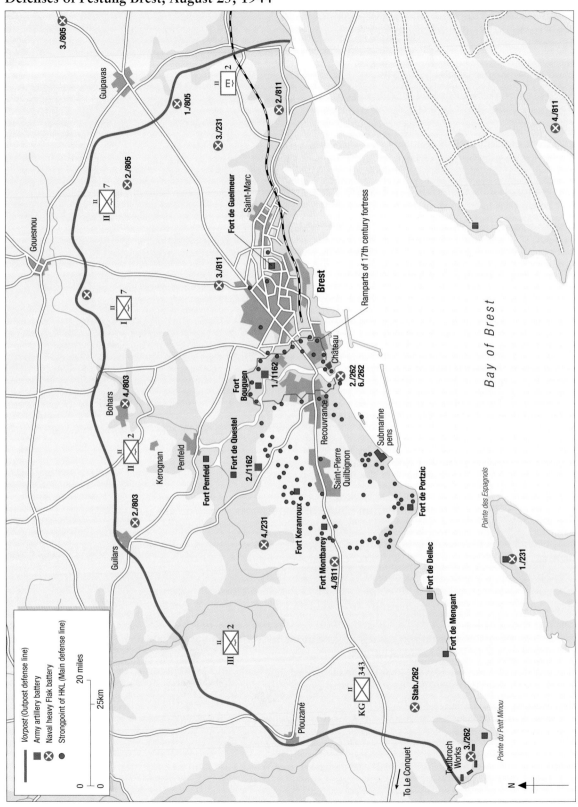

3./805

Guipavas

1./805

II | ⚔ | 7
II

2./805

II | ⚔ | 7
I

E⚔ | 2
II

2./811

3./231

3./811

Fort de Guelmeur

Saint-Marc

Brest

Ramparts of 17th century fortress

4./811

Gouesnou

4./803

Bohars

II | ⚔ | 2
II

Kerognan   Penfeld

Fort Penfeld

Fort de Questel

2./1162

Fort Bouguen

1/1162

Château

2./262
6./262

Recouvrance

Saint-Pierre
Quilbignon

Submarine
pens

Bay of Brest

2./803

Guilars

4./231

Fort Keranroux

Fort Montbarey

4./811

Fort de Portzic

Fort de Dellec

1./231

Pointe des Espagnols

II | ⚔ | 2
III

Plouzané

KG | ⚔ | 343
II

Stab./262

Fort de Mengant

Toulbroch
Works

3./262

To Le Conquet

Pointe du Petit Minou

N

Legend:
Vorpost (Outpost defense line)
■ Army artillery battery
⊗ Naval heavy Flak battery
● Strongpoint of HKL (Main defense line)

0   20 miles
0   25km

50

Flak position near the bridge, 5./M.Fla.Abt. 811. The peninsula provided an excellent vantage point overlooking the Brest harbor, and so Middleton deployed the 174th Field Artillery Group there with three artillery battalions. These played an important role in the subsequent fighting.

FESTUNG BREST

The defense of Festung Brest was led by Oberst Hans von der Mosel. However, the only troops directly under his command were several companies of Festung-Stamm-Regt. 25 assigned to various strongpoints. The remainder of the troops were under various other commands, principally Konteradmiral Otto Kähler, Seekommandant der Bretagne. Besides the city and its suburbs, Festung Brest also included the southwestern tip of Brittany around La Conquet and the defenses across the Bay of Brest on the Crozon Peninsula. In late July 1944 before the arrival of American forces in Brittany, the Brest garrison numbered about 14,500 military personnel. Of these, about 7,600 were directly involved in the defense of Brest consisting of coastal artillery batteries, naval Flak batteries, coastal and *Landfront* defenses and other combat roles. There were about 7,000 other military personnel, including about 6,300 naval personnel, who were assigned to Alarm units (*Alarmeinheiten*) for secondary defense missions. The size of the garrison substantially expanded in August when elements of the 266. Infanterie-Diviison, 343. Infanterie-Division and 2. Fallschirmjäger-Division, along with many other small units from elsewhere in western Brittany, withdrew into the Brest area as a result of the American assault. This more than doubled the size of the garrison to over 40,000 military personnel. Besides the military personnel, there were several thousand other German personnel,

T/Sgt. Johnny Yanak from Co. A, 9th Infantry, 2nd Division, peers over a hedge during the fighting on the eastern side of Brest on August 26. The 2nd Division issued a significant number of .45-cal. Thompson sub-machine guns to the rifle companies in an experiment to test their value in urban fighting. Contrary to popular movies and TV shows, the Thompson was not a common infantry weapon in 1944–45.

including police units, administrative personnel, construction workers from Organization Todt and the Reicharbeitsdienst (RAD), and other organizations. At their peak, Organization Todt and the RAD had 12,000 workers in the Brest area, of whom 4,000 were foreign forced laborers. Some of the German civilians were absorbed into the Alarm units.

Festung Brest had a substantial artillery force, but much of it was unsuited to the upcoming land campaign due its configuration for coastal defense. There had been a program to reinforce the coastal batteries of MAA 262, starting in 1943 with fully enclosed casemates. However, these offered only a limited field of fire and often prevented the batteries from firing on land targets to their rear. The Kriegsmarine 3. Flak-Brigade had five battalions including 14 105mm batteries, one twin 105mm battery, and one 128mm battery in the area; these could be used as dual purpose guns if provided with proper fire direction. The army was particularly weak in field artillery with only two batteries of war-booty French 105mm lFH.325(f), one battery of war-booty French 155mm sFH.414(f), and a single battery of German 105mm lFH. The assorted divisions which retreated into Festung Brest had little field artillery remaining. The only significant armored vehicles in Festung Brest were four self-propelled guns, probably the 47mm PaK(t) on war-booty Renault R-35 chassis, a type found in some divisional anti-tank companies.

One distinctive feature of the Brest fighting was the extensive use of improvised mines. The French navy's Pyrotechnie Saint-Nicholas was the source of most of the explosives, ranging from 75mm artillery projectiles to massive torpedo warheads. These were fitted with a variety of pressure detonators or other types of igniters, and lavishly spread around the field fortifications in the outer ring of Festung Brest defenses.

When it became apparent that the siege of Brest would soon begin, Berlin instructed Gen.Lt. Hermann Bernard Ramcke to take over command of Festung Brest; Mosel became his deputy and Oberst Hans Kroh took over command of the 2. Fallschirmjäger-Division. One of Ramcke's first actions was to order the evacuation of most of the French civilians from the city on August 13, the exception being fire-fighters and emergency service personnel. Ramcke established a radio link to neighboring US forces and the evacuation was conducted during a truce period every morning over the course of four days.

The Brest main defense belt (HKL: *Hauptkampflinie*) had been built as part of the Atlantic Wall program and was not well conceived. The HKL had a radius of only 3km from the center of the port, placing the port within enemy artillery range. It consisted of a semi-circular screen of fortified strongpoints. On the eastern side of the Penfeld River, the HKL was built within the urban area of the city. On the western side, it used a ring of old forts as its basis, interspersed with new strongpoints. It was divided into two sectors, east and west (Abschnitt Ost, West) and then into sub-sector, each with their own command bunkers.

As a result of the shortcomings of the HKL, Ramke based the defense of Brest on an outpost line (*Vorfeld*) beyond the city in the neighboring countryside. As in Normandy, the rural terrain was compartmented into small rectangles by dense *bocage*, a type of hedgerow designed to protect

A team of medics runs forward to recover a wounded tanker from a damaged M5A1 light tank on August 28 outside of Brest.

the fields from coastal wind. These created a natural form of inverted trench system. The hedgerows were adapted into an effective defense line by the paratroopers by carving numerous "fox burrows" into the base of the hedgerows, shielding the troops from artillery and mortar fire. Ramcke took advantage of the numerous Kriegsmarine fortified Flak batteries around the city to act as the skeleton of the *Vorfeld* outer defense belt. Aside from the utility of the Flak guns in combat, these batteries usually included a significant number of support bunkers that could be used to create an improvised fortified position. These bunkers helped to negate the American advantage in artillery since the defending infantry could remain in the bunkers during the preparatory artillery bombardment, and exit the bunkers to their field positions once the artillery had lifted.

Fortified hill-tops played an unusually prominent role in the fighting for Brest. Due to the terrain, they offered excellent vantage points for the defenders. This is the rear of an R667 bunker armed with a 50mm anti-tank gun. This was part of strongpoint B.47 immediately to the north of Fort Kéranroux, defended by paratroopers of the 7. and 8. Kompanien, II./FJR 2.

Ramcke decided to use the 2. Fallschirmjäger-Division as the basis for the defense of Brest. The area west of the Penfeld River was the responsibility of Fallschirmjäger-Regiment 2 under Oberstleutnant Karl Tannert while the eastern sector was the responsibility of Fallschirmjäger-Regiment 7 under Oberst Erich Pietzonka, reinforced by the divisional engineer battalion, FS-Pionier-Abt. 2. Neither regiment was large enough to cover such a large frontage, so the paratroopers were reinforced using other forces on hand, mainly naval personnel.

The 343. Infanterie-Division by this stage of the campaign was quite weak after its heavy losses fighting on the Daoulas Peninsula. Ramcke was skeptical of the quality of the troops of this unit, since most of its younger soldiers had been dispatched to Normandy and the remainder were mostly old men with medical troubles or attached *Osttruppen*. Two of its battalions were assigned to the HKL defense line inside the city, II./GR 852 in Abschnitt Ost and II./GR 898 in Abschnitt West. The remaining units were either broken up as replacements for the 2. Fallschirmjäger-Division or were deployed on the opposite side of the Bay of Brest on the Crozon Peninsula. The remnants of the 266. Infanterie-Division, reduced to barely two battalions, were deployed in the La Conquet area under Oberstleutnant Fürst to the west of Brest.

THE SIEGE OF BREST

Middleton planned to begin the assault on Festung Brest starting on August 24, but poor weather prevented the use of air support. As a result, the offensive was re-scheduled to start on the afternoon of August 25. The attack front was three divisions wide with the 29th Infantry Division on the right (eastern) flank, the 8th Infantry Division in the center (north), and the 2nd Infantry Division on the right (east). All three of these divisions had fought in the Battle of the Hedgerows on the approaches to Saint-Lô in July 1944, and so were familiar with the difficulties in conducting an advance in this type of terrain.

HMS *WARSPITE* VS. GERMAN COASTAL BATTERIES, AUGUST 25, 1944 (PP. 54–55)

The Royal Navy's old battleship HMS *Warspite* **(1)** was widely used during the Normandy and Brittany campaign to provide heavy fire support for Allied forces. On August 25, it was assigned to soften up several of the forts on the western side of the Brest defenses. *Warspite* was accompanied by Force 112 consisting of five destroyers, HMS *Fame*, *Inconstant*, *Duncan*, and *Hotspur* and HMCS *Assinibor* **(2)**. The *Warspite*'s commanding officer, Capt. M. H. A. Kelsey, was well aware that several of the German gun batteries were encased in steel-reinforced concrete casemates which even the 15in. battleship guns would have a hard time penetrating, short of a direct hit through the embrasures. Rather than engage in a pointless duel with the German batteries, Kelsey decided to fire on the targets from off the northwest coast of Brittany, out of sight of the German fire-control bunkers.

The engagement began at 1505hrs from a distance of 26km (16 miles) starting with 57 rounds against the Lochrist guns, Batterie Graf Spee. The aerial observer reported that the three exposed guns had been knocked out, but he was uncertain of the casemated gun. As a result, the *Warspite* turned its attention to the guns on the Rospects Peninsula, Batterie von Holtzendorf with a total of 47 rounds. After this, two of the old Vauban era forts were struck, Fort Kéranroux and Fort Montbarey. Around 1745hrs, geysers of water began to rise up alarmingly close to *Warspite* and its accompanying destroyers **(3)**. Contrary to the observer's report, only one of the Graf Spee guns had been damaged. It took almost two hours to clear away all the dirt and debris from the bombardment, but eventually, two of the Graf Spee guns were ready to fire. In the meantime, Kriegsmarine fire-control bunkers further up the coast had spotted *Warspite* and began feeding ballistic data back to the Graf Spee fire control bunker. The *Warspite* broke off the engagement at 1745hrs based on the instructions of an American fire-control officer. Both sides claimed victory. The naval gunfire had completely shattered Fort Kéranroux, but only damaged the other targets. Batterie Graf Spee gleefully reported back to naval headquarters in Brest that it had fought off a British squadron.

The *Vorpost* outpost line on the northeastern side of Brest was based on a line of naval Flak batteries. This is a typical example of a 105mm SKC/32 on an 88mm MPL C/30 D pedestal Flak gun mount of 1./M.Fla.Rgt. 805 near Kermeur-Coataudon on the approaches to Hill 105, called the Battery Domaine by US troops. The gun's kettle emplacement is flush to the ground, the gun is shrouded with a camouflage umbrella, and its associated ammunition and personnel bunkers are hidden. This particular site was captured by Co. F, 23rd Infantry, 2nd Infantry Division on the morning of August 29.

Middleton was able to call upon extensive fire support. Besides the 174th Field Artillery Group over on the Daoulas Peninsula, the 333rd Field Artillery Group supported the 29th Infantry Division, the 196th Field Artillery Group supported the 8th Infantry Division, and a 155mm howitzer battalion supported the 2nd Infantry Division. Each division had their usual three field artillery battalions, plus an added 105mm howitzer battalion. Middleton was also able to secure some air and naval support. The battleship HMS *Warspite* was assigned to bombard the German coastal batteries near Le Conquet and Recouvrance. RAF and USAAF bombers and fighter bombers also staged extensive bombing raids on the port and its defenses.

THE ATTACK EAST OF BREST

The 29th Infantry Division arrived in the eastern sector starting on August 22 and took up its position on the VIII Corps right flank. The attack began in the early afternoon of August 25 by the 115th Infantry on the right flank, the 116th Infantry on the left, advancing in a column of battalions. The 175th Infantry joined the attack on August 26 against one of the most strongly defended positions in the sector, Colline de Coscastel (Hill 103) to the east of Plouzané. This hill offered an excellent vantage point over the western sector of Brest, and so was prized by both sides. Initial attempts to take the hill were quickly repulsed. Indeed, the first three days of fighting by the division were largely unproductive due to the tenacity of FJR 2. As in the Normandy hedgerow fighting, this would prove to be a grinding battle of attrition. In the hopes of speeding the advance, at the end of the month there was shuffling of the regiments with the 116th Infantry being shifted to the extreme left (southern) flank in the hopes of securing the main Le Conquet–Brest road.

The attack on Hill 103 resumed on August 29–30, with the 175th finally seizing the crest with a night attack on August 30. However, it had been a very costly assault with the 1/175th Infantry reduced to 140 men and

THE BATTLE FOR HILL 103, AUGUST 26–SEPTEMBER 3, 1944 (PP. 58–59)

The defenses of the 2. Fallschirmjäger Division outside of Brest began with a *Vorpost* (Outpost) defense line. To the east of the Penfeld River, the *Vorpost* generally followed a line using Kriegsmarine Flak batteries as a "string of pearls." On the west side of the Penfeld River, the *Vorpost* generally used hills as the foundation of the defense. The *Vorpost* was situated in open countryside, much of it broken up with *bocage*. The hills offered an excellent vantage point over this terrain, enabling the defenders to bring down mortar and artillery fire on the attacking American troops. Some of these hill defenses had already been fortified earlier in 1943–44 with *Tobruks* and other small Atlantic Wall fortifications. *Tobruks* were a small type of *Ringstand* with a circular opening used for infantry heavy weapons such as machine guns and mortars. Hill 103 also had several underground concrete personnel shelters. Besides the concrete structures, the main form of defense on the hills were ordinary field fortifications. The forward edge of the hill defenses consisted of trenches with a double apron of barbed wire in front. Hill 103, locally known as Colline de Coscastel, was defended by troops of Hptm. Lohff's III./Fallschirmjäger-Regiment 2, reinforced with elements of Kompanie 13 (heavy weapons) and Kompanie 14 (anti-tank weapons) **(1)**.

The initial attack on Hill 175 was conducted by Lt. Col. Roger Whiteford's 1st Battalion, 175th Infantry Regiment, 29th Infantry Division starting on August 26. The initial attack was conducted against the northwest side of the hill through *bocage* country. The first day's attack was beaten back by small arms and machine-gun fire once the battalion had reached the hill. The attack on August 27 was supported by M4 medium tanks of Company A, 709th Tank Battalion **(2)**. This attack failed to secure the hill after the III./Fallschirmjäger-Regiment 2. threw in reinforcements. The attack on August 28 was two battalions strong, with the 1/175th Infantry attacking on the northwest side of the hill and Major Claude Melancon's 2/175th attacking up the south side. The fighting reached the German trench line and hand-to-hand combat ensued. In spite of the reinforcements, the German defenses held. The attack on August 29 attempted to swing the 3/175th Infantry behind Hill 103 after an extensive artillery bombardment. The daylight attack reached the outer edge of barbed wire but penetrated no further **(3)**. As a result, a night attack was planned, using the lead companies to place Bangalore torpedoes under the wire to create breaches. This succeeded in pushing the German paratroopers off the summit, but they took up reverse slope positions on the eastern side of the hill. This time, it was the Americans in the trenches. By this stage, the 175th Infantry had suffered 350 casualties with no replacements. Stubborn fighting continued over the next few days with a pattern of attacks and bloody counter-attacks. The stalemate wasn't broken until the morning of September 3, when the division committed another battalion, the 3/115th Infantry, which made a sweeping arc behind Hill 103 from the northwest, finally undermining the German defenses.

When II./FJR 7 abandoned Battery Domaine on the night of August 28, they left behind a small rearguard to detonate the ammunition when American troops approached. These were blown up on the morning of August 29, and this shows several GIs of Co. F, 23rd Infantry nearby after the explosion.

2/175th Infantry reduced to 175; full strength was 550 men each. Although the 175th had secured the crest of the hill, the German paratroopers were still nearby on the reverse slope. Ramcke declared that they must retake the hill "at all costs" and as a result, the hilltop was pummeled by all available German artillery, including coastal batteries and Flak guns, and subjected to repeated counter-attacks. By September 1, the hilltop was described by one officer as "a desolate waste." Efforts to push down from the hilltop were frustrated on September 2 due to the heavy casualties suffered by the 175th Infantry. The division reserve, 3/115th Infantry, was shifted to Hill 103 and had much more success on September 3, cutting off the German escape route and forcing an abandonment of the reverse slope of the hill by the German paratroopers.

Middleton had expected the battle to be over by September 1, but by that date, the *Landfront* had yet to be seriously breached. The corps artillery had enough ammunition for six days of fighting, and by early September was running out. As was the case in other divisional sectors, there was a relative lull in the fighting in the 29th Infantry Division sector for a few days while the VIII Corps restocked its depleted supply of field artillery ammunition.

THE ATTACK NORTH OF BREST

The attack in the northern sector was conducted by the 8th Infantry Division. This was one of the original formations of VIII Corps in Brittany and had been involved in the actions at Rennes in support of the 4th Armored Division earlier in the month. It was the first of the infantry divisions to arrive in the Brest area on August 17–18 and had relieved the 6th Armored Division. The division began its attack on August 25 with two of its regiments, the 13th and 28th Infantry, in front and the 121st Infantry in reserve. As in other sectors, the advance was slow due to stubborn German resistance and

A Breton Maquis of the FTP supporting the 2nd Infantry Division pose on August 16 near Kersaint to the northeast of Brest. They are armed with a considerable variety of weapons including British, French, American, and German rifles and carbines, some German machine guns and at least one Soviet DP machine gun.

the terrain difficulties. On the night of August 28–29, Cos. E and G, 28th Infantry attempted to infiltrate through German positions south of Kerloïs (Kergroas). Early in the morning, the advance was halted when the group was attacked by two German assault guns and an M4 medium tank captured from the 709th Tank Battalion the day before. The two assault guns were disabled, but the M4 caused considerable havoc after the American infantry expended its last bazooka rocket. The two companies were eventually overwhelmed by I./FJR 7 and forced to surrender. The German battalion commander, Major Reino Hamer, was later awarded the Knight's Cross for the day's action and the capture of approximately 500 American troops.

The fighting in late August involved the capture of two prominent hills on either side of the village of Keranchosen in the path of the advance. Hill 88 received its name, not from its elevation, but from the "88mm" guns on top. It was actually a German naval Flak battery with 105mm guns. To the east was Hill 80. After repeated attempts had failed, the reserve regiment, the 121st Infantry, was sent into the area, eventually reaching the crest of the hill on September 2. However, this brought down so much German artillery fire on the crest that it was abandoned. The 8th Infantry Division began preparing for an attack along the Lambezellec Ridge that ran parallel along the divisional front. As in the case of the 29th Infantry Division, there was a lull for a few days while VIII Corps waited for an ammunition re-supply.

THE ATTACK ON THE EAST SIDE OF BREST

The 2nd Infantry Division attacked the eastern side of Festung Brest. Its 9th Infantry Regiment secured portions of the Brest airfield. The numerous German fortified strongpoints presented a significant problem since the division had so many replacements who had not been taught how to use the

Battle for Brest, August 25 to September 18, 1944

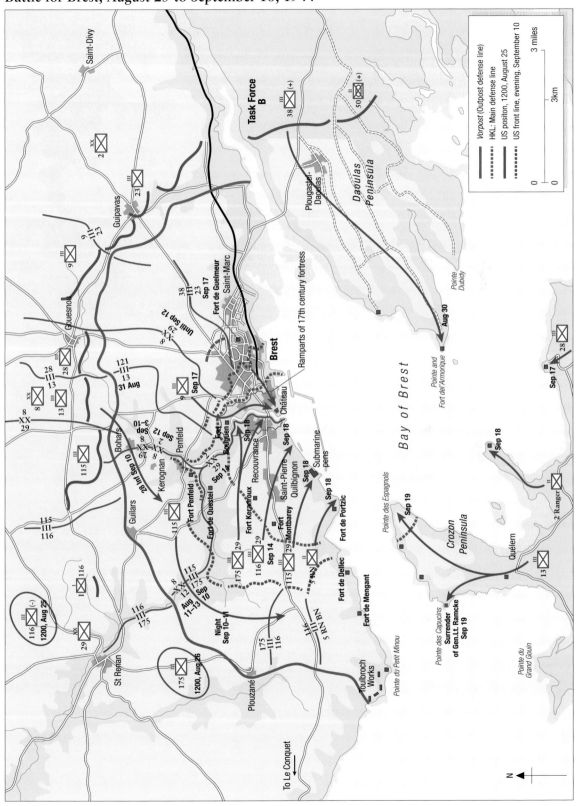

Saint-Divy

Task Force B

XX 2

III 23

Guipavas

Plougastel-Daoulas

Daoulas Peninsula

Pointe Dubidy

III 38 (+)

III 50 (+)

Vorpost (Outpost defense line)
HKL: Main defense line
US positon, 1200, August 25
US front line, evening, September 10

3 miles

3km

III 23

III 9

Gouesnou

III 9

III 28 13

XX 8 13

III 13

Bohars

III 115

Guilars

Kerognan

XX 8 29

XX 8 29

Penfeld

Fort Penfeld

III 115

Fort de Guelmeur
Saint-Marc
Sep 17

III 38 23
Sep 17

Until Sep 12

Sep 12

121 III 13
31 Aug

Sep 17

Château
Brest

Ramparts of 17th century fortress

Fort Bouguen

Sep 18

Recouvrance

Saint-Pierre
Quilbignon

Submarine pens

Sep 18

Fort de Portzic

Sep 18

Bay of Brest

Pointe and Fort del Armorique

Aug 30

III 28
Sep 17

XX 8 29

115 III 116

I 116

III 115

Fort de Questel

Fort Keranroux

Sep 18

Fort Montbarey

XX 8 12 Sep 10

115 175

115 III 175

III 29

116 29
Sep 14

III 29

Fort de Delfec

5 RN BN

5 RN BN

Fort de Mengant

Night Sep 10-11

III 116 175

175 116

Toulbroch Works

Pointe du Petit Minou

III 116 (-)
1200, Aug 25

XX 29

St Renán

III 175
1200, Aug 26

Plouzané

To Le Conquet

Pointe des Espagnols

Sep 19

Crozon Peninsula

Surrender of Gen.Lt. Ramcke
Sep 19

Pointe des Capucins

Pointe du Grand Gouin

Sep 18

II 2 Ranger

III 13

Quélern

N

63

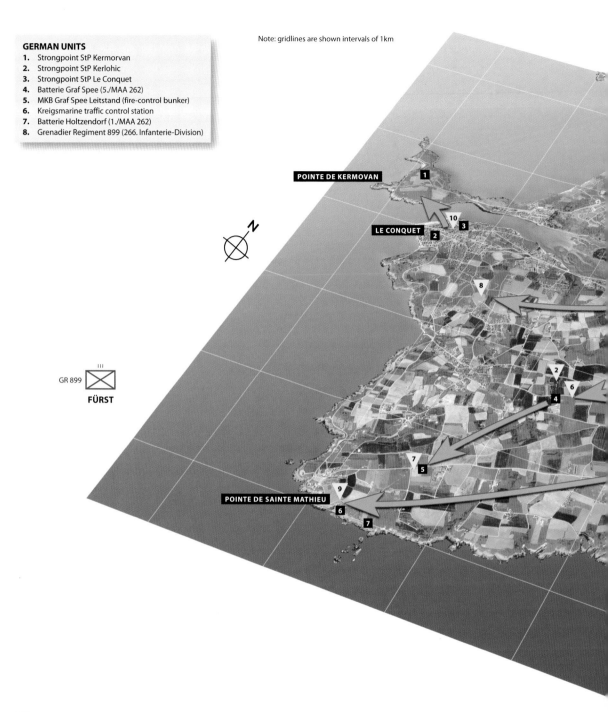

GERMAN UNITS
1. Strongpoint StP Kermorvan
2. Strongpoint StP Kerlohic
3. Strongpoint StP Le Conquet
4. Batterie Graf Spee (5./MAA 262)
5. MKB Graf Spee Leitstand (fire-control bunker)
6. Kreigsmarine traffic control station
7. Batterie Holtzendorf (1./MAA 262)
8. Grenadier Regiment 899 (266. Infanterie-Division)

Note: gridlines are shown intervals of 1km

POINTE DE KERMOVAN

LE CONQUET

GR 899 ⊠
FÜRST

POINTE DE SAINTE MATHIEU

▼ EVENTS

1. August 30: the 2nd Rangers capture Hill 63, a high point overlooking Le Conquet.

2 August 31: Batterie Graf Spee begins bombarding the 2nd Rangers.

3 September 1: Battery C, 227th Field Artillery Battalion begins counter-battery fire on Batterie Graf Spee.

4 September 3: the 2nd Rangers stages attack toward Batterie Graf Spee but is forced back by heavy fire.

5 September 6: the 3/116th Infantry joins the attack, reaches Hill 53.

6 September 8: Batterie Graf Spee has its guns disabled by artillery fire and air attack and falls to an attack by the 2nd Rangers.

7 September 8: A patrol by 1Lt. Robert Edlin of Co. A, 2nd Rangers captures the "Man Made Mound", the fire-control battery of Graf Spee, along with the sector commander Obst. Fürst.

8 September 8: the 5th Rangers begin attack on La Conquet, clearing the two strongpoints by September 9.

9 September 9: Company L, 3/116th Infantry take the naval control station on Pointe de Sainte Mathieu.

10 September 10: the 5th Rangers plan amphibious raid against Stützpunkt Kermorvan, but an attack by P-47 Thunderbolts convinces the garrison to surrender.

11 September 10: the 3/116th Infantry clear out a German detachment in the Hotel des Bains with tank support from the 709th Tank Battalion.

64

TASK FORCE SUGAR ATTACKS THE LE CONQUET SECTOR

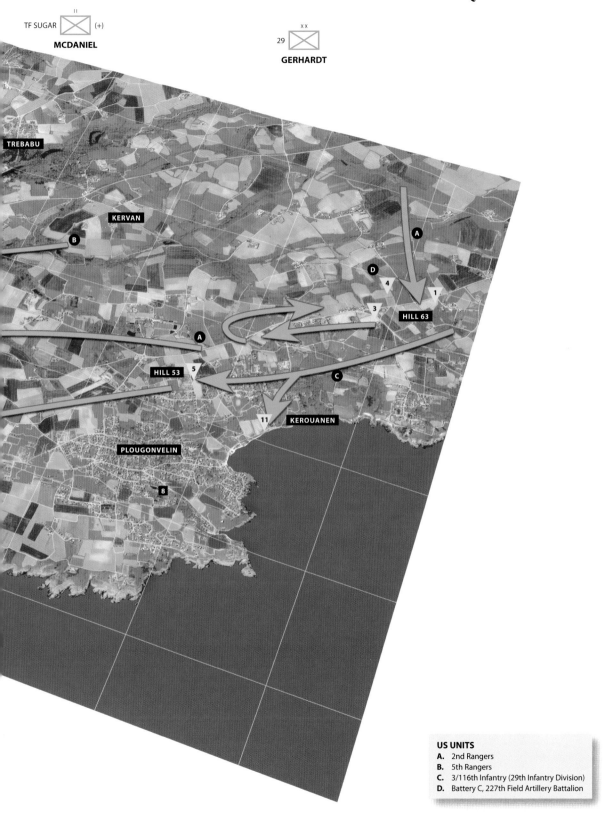

TF SUGAR (+)
MCDANIEL

29
GERHARDT

TREBABU

KERVAN

B

A

D
4

3

1

HILL 63

A

HILL 53
5

C

11   KEROUANEN

PLOUGONVELIN

8

US UNITS
A. 2nd Rangers
B. 5th Rangers
C. 3/116th Infantry (29th Infantry Division)
D. Battery C, 227th Field Artillery Battalion

various close-assault weapons such as flame-throwers, Bangalore torpedoes, and pole-and-satchel charges that were essential in this type of fighting. In the 23rd Infantry sector, the main objective was the fortified Hill 105, defended by Major Becker's II./FJR 7. The site was shielded by a 105mm Flak battery, 1./M.Fla.Abt. 805 called Battery Domaine by the US troops. Hill 105 had been attacked, without success, by the 50th Armored Infantry Battalion of the 6th Armored Division in the initial phase of the battle on August 12. After the survivors of Battery Domaine withdrew on the night of August 28, a small rearguard detonated the ammunition bunkers on the morning of August 29, causing extensive casualties among the lead squads of the 23rd Infantry. Further to the north, the 3/9th Infantry took four days to overcome a set of German field fortifications around the Bourg-Neuf and Four-Neuf area, later being awarded the Presidential Unit Citation for the costly action. This opened up a gap in the outer layer of defenses on the northern side of Festung Brest. These actions were the first to crack open the outer defenses of Festung Brest, and the 2nd Infantry Division took advantage of this by pushing into the Saint-Marc suburbs on the eastern side of Brest. By this stage of the fighting, the 2nd Infantry Division noted the decreasing number of German paratroopers encountered, and the greater reliance on poorly trained and poorly led naval infantry. This was in large measure due to the heavy attrition suffered by FJR 7 in the first week of fighting.

TASK FORCE SUGAR, AUGUST 30 TO SEPTEMBER 10

The attack by the 29th Infantry Division was complicated by the fact that there was a substantial German force on the southwestern coast of Brittany around Le Conquet, including a great deal of coastal artillery. Due to its suitability for amphibious landings, the Germans had heavily fortified the Le Conquet area with four integrated strongpoints, Stützpunkt Kerlouchan, Stützpunkt Kermorvan, Stützpunkt Le Conquet and Stützpunkt Kerlohic. Behind these was the powerful Marine-Küsten-Batterie Graf Spee (5./MAA

Three of the four 280mm SKL/40 guns of Batterie Graf Spee were still in open kettle pits, and so could be used to fire against the advancing 2nd Rangers. It engaged in a duel with the Royal Navy battleship HMS *Warspite* on the afternoon of August 25, without either side scoring any fatal hits.

262) armed with four 280mm SK L/40 naval guns. The southern tip of Brittany at Saint-Mathieu had a fortified naval fire control position and there was an associated naval coastal battery, MKB von Holtzendorf, armed with four 150mm SK C/28 naval guns on the neighboring Rospects Peninsula. The forces in this sector were led by Oberstleutnant Martin Fürst, commander of GR 899 of the 266. Infanterie-Division, and consisted mainly of survivors from this division along with assorted Kriegsmarine units, totaling more than 2,000 troops.

Since the 29th Infantry Division was preoccupied with the attack eastward into Brest, Middleton decided to delegate the mission against Le Conquet to his Special Forces units, the 2nd and 5th Rangers. These were used to create Task Force S (Sugar). It was commanded by Col. Edward McDaniel, the 29th Infantry Division chief of staff in order to better coordinate actions with the 29th Infantry Division. Both Ranger battalions were understrength since their well-known actions on D-Day at Pointe-du-Hoc and Omaha Beach. Task Force Sugar, even with its attachments, was barely a reinforced battalion with only 1,300 men. It faced enemy forces more than twice their size, protected by heavily fortified positions.

The attack began on August 30 with the 2nd Rangers capturing Hill 63, a high point overlooking Le Conquet. The Graf Spee battery had been firing at 29th Infantry Division positions for several days, including several hits in the divisional headquarters area. As a result, Battery C, 227th Field Artillery Battalion with four 155mm howitzers was dispatched to Task Force Sugar to begin counter-battery preparations. The gun batteries engaged in duels through early September. The 2nd Rangers, under Col. James Rudder, attempted to assault the Graf Spee battery on September 3, but his small force was hit by direct fire from the battery and forced to withdraw back to Hill 63. Rudder was reinforced by the 3/116th Infantry and staged another assault on September 6–7, finally reaching Hills 53 and 54 in the foreground to the battery.

The 29th Infantry Division commander, Maj. Gen. Charles Gerhardt, was impatient with the slow progress, and replaced McDaniel with the assistant divisional commander, Col. Leroy Watson. Task Force Sugar was gradually

The fire-control bunker for Batterie Graf Spee was built on an artificial hill near Trovern for better observation. The 2nd Rangers dubbed it the "Man Made Mound" while the Germans called it variously the *Termitenhügel* (Termite mound) or *Pilzhöhle* (Mushroom cave). The commander for the Le Conquet sector, Obstlt. Martin Fürst had established his command post here on August 11 and was captured here by a patrol led by 1Lt. Robert Edlin of Co. A, 2nd Rangers. This site was converted into a museum in 2017.

reinforced with some modest tank and artillery support which assisted the 3/116th Infantry in securing the Saint-Mathieu area. The Graf Spee battery had been significantly weakened by air and artillery attack and was finally overrun by Rudder's 2nd Rangers on September 8.

A patrol by 1Lt. Robert Edlin of Co. A, 2nd Rangers encountered the battery's fire-control bunker near Trovern and the three Rangers made their way inside. Edlin demanded to see the commander, who turned out to be Oberst Fürst, the sector commander. Edlin insisted that Fürst surrender, but Fürst refused and told Edlin that he and his patrol was now his prisoners. Edlin took a grenade, pulled the pin, put it against Fürst's abdomen and told him "You're either going to surrender or die now!". Startled by Edlin's intensity, Fürst agreed to surrender. He would not submit to an officer of lower rank, so Edlin requested Rudder to join him for a formal surrender. Rudder attempted to convince Fürst to order the surrender of the Le Conquest garrison, which he refused.

The 5th Rangers began attacks into Stützpunkt Le Conquet on September 8–9, quickly reducing the defenses against dispirited resistance. On September 10, the 5th Rangers prepared an amphibious assault across the inlet to attack the neighboring Stützpunkt Kermorvan, but a strafing attack by P-47 Thunderbolts led to the surrender of the garrison in the late afternoon before the attack was launched. The final defensive work in the area, Stützpunkt Kerlouchan, was remote enough that Task Force Sugar decided to contain "the Old Fort" using a French resistance group of about 70 former Soviet troops of Ost-Bataillon 633 who had defected with the persuasion of Jedburgh Team Horace on the Daoulas Peninsula at the end of August. In the event, the isolated garrison of 50 German troops decided to surrender rather than face the bloody retribution of the French/Russian Maquis.

THE BREST OFFENSIVE RESUMES

An infantry patrol of the 2nd Infantry Division moves along Rue de la Duchesse Anne in Saint-Marc on the eastern side of Brest on September 9, 1944.

Patton's Third US Army had expected Brest to fall quickly, and as a result, provided very modest artillery ammunition supplies to VIII Corps. Shortages began to become manifest by August 29, and had become acute by September 5–6. The situation was exacerbated by the growing distance between VIII Corps and the rest of the Third US Army, which was now heading towards Lorraine, some 570 miles away (915km). The command problem was solved a few days later when VIII Corps was broken off from Patton's Third US Army and attached instead to the newly arrived Ninth US Army under Lt. Gen. William Simpson, though this had no immediate effect on the ammunition problem.

Middleton explained the urgency of the ammunition crisis to Bradley, and finally eight LSTs were sent with a substantial amount of artillery

ammunition. These were landed at Saint-Michel-en-Grève near Morlaix. The availability of adequate ammunition supplies had an immediate effect on the fighting.

The offensive was resumed on September 8 by all three divisions with considerable fire support from the newly replenished field artillery. While only 1,000 prisoners had been captured through September 8, on September 9 alone, some 2,500 prisoners were taken. The 2/115th Infantry, 29th Infantry Division finally pushed through the Kerognan (Kerrognant) strongpoint, a fortified battery position of 4./M.Fla.Abt. 805 that was being defended by II./FJR 2. This attack was significantly aided by several tanks from the 709th Tank Battalion. Late in the day, the regiment occupied Fort Penfeld, which had been abandoned by FJR 2.

When the offensive was renewed on September 8, the 2nd Infantry Division was on the verge of entering the urbanized region of Brest, starting with the eastern suburb of Saint-Marc, defended by II./FJR 7 and the FS.Pionier-Abt. 2. They began to encounter the first element of Brest HKL defense belt, a cluster of three strongpoints in the eastern side of Saint-Marc. These were constructed around major road and street intersections and consisted of *Ringstands*, a type of small bunker with a circular opening for a machine gun or mortar. These strongpoints often included a *Ringstand* with a tank turret, able to cover the entire intersection against approaching armored vehicles. The fighting in Saint-Marc was house-to-house. The three regiments of the 2nd Infantry Division were supported by a variety of weapons including both towed and self-propelled tank destroyers, and a few M12 155mm GMC self-propelled guns. The division's engineers provided vital support in the form of explosive charges, used to blow entrances between buildings. A 2nd Infantry Division history recalled the fighting for Saint-Marc:

> The advance was now a macabre dance of death in a doomed city. The streets were grim deathtraps, swept by machine gun and flak fire from guns set up at street intersections. They were empty and silent until a gun cracked, a machine

gun chattered, a shell descended and burst. At night parachute flares went up, making the scene even more eerie. The men of the Division advanced by swarming over fences, up ladders, across improvised catwalks across the rooftops among the chimney-pots. They slipped over garden walls and through kitchen doors, or scaled walls and attacked from the roof to the cellar to keep the Nazis from retreating to the top story and showering them with rifle fire and grenades.

The 9th Infantry in the north and the 38th Infantry in the center were the first to reach the outer walls of the old city of Brest on September 14. The 23rd Infantry, fighting on the southern side along the edge of the port, began reaching the wall on September 15. Scout patrols found an unguarded railroad tunnel into the city and quickly began to infiltrate past the old city walls via the railroad station. This largely signaled the end of coherent defenses on the northern and eastern side of Brest, though much house-to-house fighting remained over the next few days to mop up small hold-out detachments.

As the three divisions closed in on Brest, there was some reorganization. The 115th Infantry was pinched out and moved to the southern (right) flank of the 29th Infantry Division, with the 8th Infantry Division taking over this sector of the front on the night of September 10–11. Middleton decided that two divisions would be enough for the final fighting inside Brest, and so the 8th Infantry Division was pinched out a regiment at a time through September 13. At this point, the 29th Infantry Division was responsible for the sector west of the Penfeld River, and the 2nd Infantry Division for the sector to the east.

At the time the offensive resumed on September 8, the German garrison, and especially the 2. Fallschirmjäger-Division, had suffered crippling attrition. II./FJR 7 which had borne the brunt of the attacks by the 2nd Infantry Division, had been largely overwhelmed, and the battalion commander, Major Becker, was captured on September 8 along with much of his staff. The replacement pool of naval personnel was almost dry and on September 8, the defenders in the eastern sector received an army postal unit of 18 men led by a 69-year-old postmaster, along with the 30 men of the paratroop division band. On September 9, the reserves were finally exhausted when the last group of naval accountants were sent into the line as infantry. US interrogation of prisoners revealed that "morale is very low among attached naval personnel, and they are not inclined to fight, but are kept in line with threats by paratroop officers and NCOs. A sailor impressed into 7./FJR 7 and remarked that the American "propaganda leaflets may have accomplished a great deal, but the machine pistol of Oberluetnant Stortz is more powerful!" A paratrooper prisoner complained that "paratroops are being used more as police to keep navy personnel in line than anything else."

An M4 medium tank of the 709th Tank Battalion passes along Rue de Bohars in the town of Lambézellec on September 9, 1944 while supporting the 8th Infantry Division on the northern side of Brest. The tank is fitted with a Rhino hedge-cutter device, a modification introduced for Operation *Cobra* in late July 1944.

FORT MONTBAREY

The geography of the defenses in the 29th Infantry Division sector was significantly different from those facing the 2nd Infantry Division. The outer edge of the *Hauptkampflinie* was still out in the countryside, delineated by a string of old forts. The two most significant of these were Fort Montbarey and Fort Kéranroux, defended by elements of Major Ewald's II./Fallschirmjäger-Regiment 2. Major-General Gerhardt, the 29th Infantry Division commander, decided to deal with Fort Kéranroux first, using the 175th Infantry. By this stage, the fort had been substantially damaged by bombing attack and gunfire from HMS *Warspite*. It was overcome on September 13 against very modest resistance.

One of the main strongpoints on the western side of Brest was Fort Montbarey, completed in 1784. The earth-filled masonry ramparts were 40ft thick and the fort was surrounded by a moat fifteen feet deep and about 40ft wide.

Fort Montbarey, held by 6./FJR 2 under Oberleutnant Flöter, proved to be a much more difficult objective. The garrison inside the fort was modest – about 200 men – but the fort was very resistant to artillery fire. In addition, the fort was protected by a minefield that included improvised mines made from 300-pound torpedo warheads. Due to a lack of American flamethrower tanks, Montgomery's 21st Army Group provided B Squadron, 141 RAC, equipped with Churchill Crocodile flamethrower tanks.

The first attack on September 15 isolated the fort, but failed to overcome its defenses. Under very difficult circumstances, Company B, 121st Engineer Combat Battalion had cleared narrow paths through the minefield. When three Crocodiles approached the fort, one struck one of the 300-pound improvised mines and was completely destroyed. The leading Churchill commanded by Lt. Tony Ward had almost made it past the fort to the town

Fifteen Churchill Crocodile flamethrower tanks of B Squadron, 141 RAC were sent to VIII Corps to assist in the reduction of German fortifications in the Brest area, starting with Fort Montbarey on September 15–17.

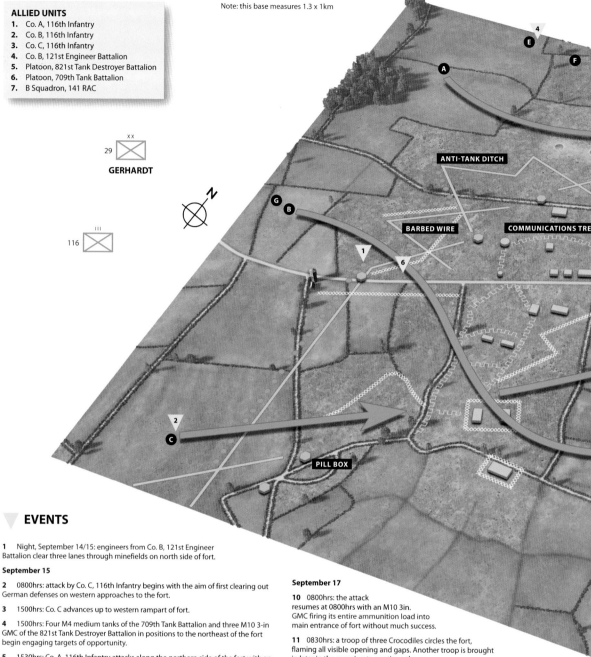

ALLIED UNITS

1. Co. A, 116th Infantry
2. Co. B, 116th Infantry
3. Co. C, 116th Infantry
4. Co. B, 121st Engineer Battalion
5. Platoon, 821st Tank Destroyer Battalion
6. Platoon, 709th Tank Battalion
7. B Squadron, 141 RAC

Note: this base measures 1.3 x 1km

29 ⊠ xx

GERHARDT

116 ⊠ III

ANTI-TANK DITCH

BARBED WIRE

COMMUNICATIONS TRE

PILL BOX

▼ EVENTS

1 Night, September 14/15: engineers from Co. B, 121st Engineer Battalion clear three lanes through minefields on north side of fort.

September 15

2 0800hrs: attack by Co. C, 116th Infantry begins with the aim of first clearing out German defenses on western approaches to the fort.

3 1500hrs: Co. C advances up to western rampart of fort.

4 1500hrs: Four M4 medium tanks of the 709th Tank Battalion and three M10 3-in GMC of the 821st Tank Destroyer Battalion in positions to the northeast of the fort begin engaging targets of opportunity.

5 1530hrs: Co. A, 116th Infantry attacks along the northern side of the fort with an aim of cutting off the eastern side.

6 1600hrs: Co. B attacks with three Churchill Crocodiles. Lt. Ward's lead Crocodile makes it through the minefield but the following tank runs over a mine and the third tank is blocked in the process. After a path is cleared, one more Crocodile and two US M4 tanks move into the area, but become trapped in deep craters.

7 1630hrs: Ward's Crocodile flames the north side of the wall, and then does the same on the south side until its fuel is exhausted.

8 1800hrs: Co. B, 116th Infantry follows behind Ward's Crocodile and eventually reaches the eastern side of the fort by early evening. A total of 122 German prisoners are taken during the fighting that day.

September 16

9 The 121st Engineers bring in an armored bulldozer to help clear more paths through the minefield on the northern side. Additional engineer preparations are made for the follow-on attack the next day.

September 17

10 0800hrs: the attack resumes at 0800hrs with an M10 3in. GMC firing its entire ammunition load into main entrance of fort without much success.

11 0830hrs: a troop of three Crocodiles circles the fort, flaming all visible opening and gaps. Another troop is brought in later in the morning to continue the process.

12 1000hrs: two more M10 3in. GMC are brought forward, and one blasts open a hole in a tunnel at the base of the northern moat. The commander of the 1/116th, Major Tom Dallas, asks the engineers to bring up as much explosives as possible to pack the tunnel and collapse the north rampart.

13 1300hrs: a 105mm howitzer from the 116th Cannon Company is placed point blank to the fort entrance and begins battering the door with high explosive and white phosphorus, eventually creating a gap.

14 1330hrs: a Churchill tank pulled up in front of the door and fires 86 rounds of high explosive into the fort.

15 1400hrs: impatient with another parley with the Germans, Dallas orders the engineers to detonate a 2,000-pound explosive charge they had secreted in the tunnel under the north wall.

16 Late afternoon: stunned by the enormous explosive blast, the Germans waited for the tank fire to quiet and began surrendering.

FORT MONTBAREY, SEPTEMBER 15, 1944

MINES

FLÖTER

FORT MONTBAREY

GERMAN UNITS
1. Fort Montbarey
2. 6./Fallschirmjäger-Regiment 2
   (Oberleutnant Flöter)

An M18 76mm GMC named "Big Gee" of Co. B, 705th Tank Destroyer Battalion waits on Rue Kerfautras while supporting 3/38th Infantry, 2nd Division in the fighting around the Saint-Martin church on September 12. These tanks destroyers were widely used in the Brest fighting for attacking reinforced strongpoints.

of Recouvrance on the eastern outskirts of Brest before becoming trapped in a crater; Gerhardt later recommended Ward for the US Army's Silver Star for "intrepidity."

After further engineer efforts to widen the gap in the minefield, the attack resumed on September 17. The fort was masked using mortar and artillery smoke rounds. Three Crocodiles approached to the edge of the moat to begin attacking the fort apertures with flame. An engineer team placed 2,000 pounds of explosive at the base of the fort's north wall. Tank destroyers and a 105mm cannon of the 116th Infantry Cannon Company pounded the main gate at pointblank range. The explosive charge was detonated in the late afternoon, collapsing a portion of the north ramparts. Many Germans were stunned by the blast, but hesitated to surrender due to continued firing by

A 3in. antitank gun of the 612th Tank Destroyer Battalion provides fire support for the 2nd Infantry Division during the fighting in Brest on September 17. This gun was positioned on the high ground near the Ker-Stears château overlooking the port and the railway station evident to the right.

a Churchill tank into the courtyard of the fort. After the firing stopped, US infantry and engineers proceeded into the fort through the gap in the wall and German troops began surrendering. There were about 75 German survivors.

Combined with the debilitating attrition of FJR 2, the removal of Fort Montbarey from the main defense line cracked open the western side of the Festung Brest defenses. The situation became so serious that Ramcke himself led a desperate counter-attack, riding one of the last surviving assault guns. The attack force was made up primarily from the 5. and 6. Kompanie of FJR 2 and was led by Oberleutnant Erich Lepkowski. Under heavy artillery fire, the assault gun broke down. Ramcke dismounted, only to suffer from a near miss in which he was "blown through the air for several yards, but jumped up and continued to give orders." An officer accompanying him

The old fort north of Fort Montbarey, Fort Kéranroux, was so badly damaged by naval gunfire from the Royal Navy battleship HMS *Warspite* on August 25 that German resistance to the advance of the 29th Infantry Division here was negligible.

ATTACK ON FORT MONTBAREY SEPTEMBER 15–17, 1944 (PP. 76–77)

The numerous fortified positions around Brest had prompted Maj. Gen. Middleton to request flamethrower tanks. Since there were no US Army flamethrower tanks in service yet, they were provided in the form of the British Churchill Crocodile flamethrower tanks **(1)**. These were based on the Churchill VII, with a flame gun fitted in place of the bow machine gun along with a special trailer for 400-gallons of fuel and compressed air. The flame-gun could fire almost five gallons of fuel per second to a range of about 100 yards and usually fired in bursts of several seconds. The detachment sent to Brest was Major Nigel "Tony" Ryle's B Squadron, 141st RAC with 15 Crocodiles, three normal gun tanks and a command tank.

During the first attack on September 15, three Crocodiles led by Lt. Hubert "Tony" Ward passed through a minefield cleared the previous night by the 121st Engineer Battalion. The soil had been so badly churned up by constant artillery fire and bombing that some of the German mines had been missed. The second

Churchill through the line hit a buried 300-pound torpedo warhead, killing the driver and injuring the rest of the crew. The third Crocodile was blocked as a result, only being freed later in the day. Ward's Crocodile proceeded to expend its entire flame contents on the embrasures and other openings visible on the fort walls **(2)**. The first day's attack breached the outer defenses of the fort but failed to secure the surrender of the garrison.

After additional engineer activity to clear paths through the minefields, the attack resumed on September 17 with an attack by three Crocodiles under Capt. Roy Moss. The flamethrowers helped demoralize the German garrison, but they could not breach the thick fort walls. With their fuel expended, they proceeded to attack the fort with their 75mm guns. Eventually, a 2,000-pound charge was placed in a tunnel under the northern wall of the fort. When detonated, it collapsed a large portion of the wall, allowing the 116th Infantry to enter the fort. In the event, the German garrison finally surrendered.

was killed and Lepkowski was seriously wounded. The counter-attack failed and Ramcke was escorted back to the main command bunker near the Marineschüle and submarine pens. By late in the day, the 116th and 175th Infantry had reached the outer walls of the old city in the Recouvrance area, and soon were inside the city walls.

While the 29th Infantry Division was attacking the western side of the Brest defenses, the 5th Rangers had been assigned to clear out the numerous coastal forts further south along the Bay of Brest. The "Battle of the Forts" took ten days, ending with the capitulation of Fort du Portzic on September 18. Most of these old forts could play little role in the final defense of Brest, but there were small garrisons in most of them.

FESTUNG BREST SURRENDERS

By nightfall on September 15, it was clear that Festung Brest was on the verge of collapse. Gen.Lt. Ramcke decided to depart Brest to continue the fight from the nearby Crozon Peninsula. Ramcke and his staff left by boat after dark on the evening of September 16, leaving his deputy, Gen.Maj. Hans von der Mosel, in charge of the city defenses.

Once the 2nd and 29th Infantry Divisions had fought their way into the walled section of the city, the German defenses largely collapsed. The improvised German naval units did not have the tenacity or fighting prowess of the paratroopers. The surrender of Festung Brest was disjointed. The city defenses east of the Penfeld River was led by Oberst Erich Pietzonka, commander of Fallschirmjäger-Regiment 7. In the early afternoon of September 18, he sent an emissary forward under a white flag, meeting American troops on Rue Émile. Major Kernan of the 9th Infantry accompanied the emissary to Pietzonka's command bunker near Place Wilson, where they discussed the terms of surrender. Later in the afternoon, Pietzonka handed over his pistol to Maj. Gen. Robertson, the 2nd Division commander, on Place Wilson.

In the 29th Division sector, the 115th Infantry had fought its way to the edge of the port and within site of the large submarine bunkers. The open ground near the submarine bunkers and the adjacent naval academy

The old city of Brest was surrounded by substantial fortress ramparts. These were reinforced with modern defenses as part of the Atlantic Wall program. This is the Arsenal on the eastern side of the city walls, fortified at strongpoint B18 with four R669 gun casemates of 1./HAA 1162, each armed with a 105mm lFH 325 (f). This area was captured by the 29th Infantry Division in the final fighting.

The Château de Brest was built by Vauban starting in 1631 to protect the Brest roadstead and access into the Penfeld River. It served as strongpoint B370 under German occupation, being used by the harbor commander. It was captured by the 2nd Infantry Division on September 18, 1944. Rebuilt after the war, it now serves as a maritime museum.

The senior commanders of Festung Brest surrendered to the 115th Infantry, 29th Infantry Division near their command bunker in the submarine pens. Here, they are seen being escorted away with *Festung* commander Gen.Maj. Hans von der Mosel on the left, Brest naval commander Konteradmiral Otto Kähler in the center, and 2. Fallschirmjäger-Division commander Hans Kroh on the right.

was dotted with the armored cupolas of buried bunkers, and rather than waste men trying to advance across the gap, an M12 155mm GMC self-propelled gun was brought up to fire against the defenses. Sporadic firing continued through September 18 until about 0745hrs hours when Co. E, 115th Infantry reported a party of German officers approaching under a white flag. The surrender party wanted a token force to take over the command bunker near the Marineschüle (naval academy) where Gen.Maj. Mosel and the rest of senior German commanders were stationed. The division headquarters ordered all firing to stop at 0900hrs, but fighting continued in the area until 1025hrs. A white flag went up over the submarine pens and the Germans garrison began filing out. The process took hours as there were thousands of naval personnel in the many bunkers and other structures in the harbor area.

German casualties in the battle for Brest had been about 4,000 killed, and 37,888 prisoners. Of the prisoners, there were about 7,900 wounded. American casualties in VIII Corps had been 9,831 men.

THE BATTLE FOR THE CROZON PENINSULA

The final fighting for the Brest area took place on the Crozon Peninsula on the opposite side of the Bay of Brest. This sector was held primarily by the 343. Infanterie-Division which by mid-

September had been reduced to three weak *Ost* battalions assigned to the neck of the peninsula near Crozon. The northern sector was defended by a detachment of 170 paratroopers of FJR 7 sent by boat to the Pointe des Espagnols opposite the Brest harbor on the evening of September 13. There were about 8,000 German personnel in the area in mid-September, including naval coastal artillery crews and other assorted troops, but very few infantry troops.

The Crozon Peninsula had been cut off on August 27 by a cavalry squadron of Task Force B while the main operations were taking place on the neighboring Daoulas Peninsula. This task force was subsequently replaced by Task Force A. To seal off the peninsula, Maj. Gen. Earnest decided to attack Hill 330, which also gained a useful observation post over the peninsula. After this hill was captured, Task Force A took up defensive positions and conducted patrols to contain the trapped German forces. When the 8th Infantry Division was squeezed out of the Brest fighting in the second week of September, it was transferred to the Crozon Peninsula along with Rudder's 2nd Rangers to capture the rest of the peninsula.

Gen.Lt. Ramcke was cornered on the Pointe des Capucins on the afternoon of September 19 by the 8th Infantry Division. He and his staff were sent to the division headquarters for the formal surrender.

On September 17, the 8th Infantry Division liberated the towns of Crozon and Morgat after overrunning the 343. Infanterie-Division's main line of resistance, II./Ost-Mitte and Ost-Battaillon 800. The southern sector of the peninsula was mopped up on September 18 and the divisional command post on Cap de la Chévre surrendered that day.

The 13th Infantry was assigned to deal with the defenses on the northern peninsula. On September 19, the assault groups scaled a wall across the peninsula south of the Quélern Fort. They mopped up resistance on the peninsula during the morning. Ramcke had his command post in a bunker on the Pointe des Capucins, and sent out emissaries. The emissary reached the assistant division commander, Brig. Gen. Charles Canham. The message asked for the commanding officer's credentials, to which Canham replied that "his troops were his credentials." Ramcke ordered an assault gun near the command post to fire its last round, at which point he agreed to surrender in the afternoon. Although this ended the fighting on the Crozon Peninsula, there was still an isolated German garrison of about 300 troops at Douarnenez on the bay south of Crozon. Task Force A sent a detachment there on September 20, and when they refused to surrender, they were quickly persuaded by a short artillery barrage.

The fighting for the Crozon Peninsula cost the US forces 72 killed and 415 wounded; there were 7,638 German prisoners taken. This ended the battle for Festung Brest.

THE LAST BASTIONS

At the beginning of August 1944, the capture of Brest and the other Breton ports around the Quiberon Bay had been a strategic priority for Allied planners. Yet within a month, the strategic situation had changed completely.

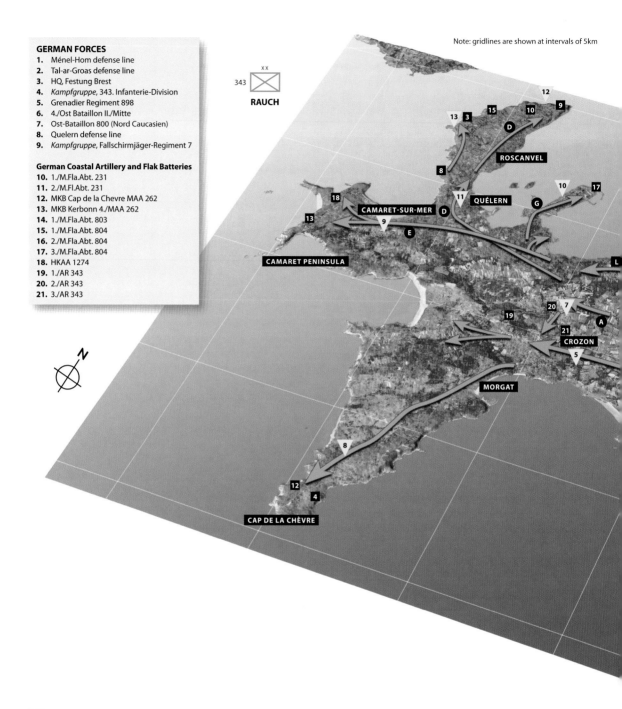

Note: gridlines are shown at intervals of 5km

GERMAN FORCES
1. Ménel-Hom defense line
2. Tal-ar-Groas defense line
3. HQ, Festung Brest
4. *Kampfgruppe,* 343. Infanterie-Division
5. Grenadier Regiment 898
6. 4./Ost Bataillon II./Mitte
7. Ost-Bataillon 800 (Nord Caucasien)
8. Quelern defense line
9. *Kampfgruppe,* Fallschirmjäger-Regiment 7

German Coastal Artillery and Flak Batteries
10. 1./M.Fla.Abt. 231
11. 2./M.Fl.Abt. 231
12. MKB Cap de la Chevre MAA 262
13. MKB Kerbonn 4./MAA 262
14. 1./M.Fla.Abt. 803
15. 1./M.Fla.Abt. 804
16. 2./M.Fla.Abt. 804
17. 3./M.Fla.Abt. 804
18. HKAA 1274
19. 1./AR 343
20. 2./AR 343
21. 3./AR 343

RAUCH

ROSCANVEL

CAMARET-SUR-MER

QUÉLERN

CAMARET PENINSULA

CROZON

MORGAT

CAP DE LA CHÈVRE

▼ **EVENTS**

1 August 23: FFI units take up position at base of peninsula.

2 August 27: US cavalry squadrons patrol the base of the peninsula.

3 September 3: Task Force A pushes up the peninsula past Telgruc and establishes a blocking position.

4 September 15: units from the 8th Infantry Division arrive on the Crozon Peninsula and prepare to assault through the German defense line.

5 September 17: 121st Infantry supported by the FFI liberate Crozon.

6 September 17: 28th Infantry pushes past German defenses along coast.

7 September 17: Task Force A pushes into the Crozon Peninsula, then heads south.

8 September 18: Task Force A pushes south to Cap de la Chèvre and accepts the surrender of Gen.Lt. Rauch and the headquarters of the 343. Infanterie-Division.

9 September 18: 28th Infantry advances into the Camaret Peninsula, clears it by the 19th.

10 September 18: 2nd Rangers pushes over the Le Fret Peninsula to Ile Longue.

11 September 18: 13th Infantry reaches the fortified line near Quélern by the evening.

12 September 18: 13th Infantry attacks the old Quélern fort and clears the last hold-outs from FJR 7 on the Pointe des Espagnols.

13 September 19: Gen.Lt. Ramcke surrenders to the 8th Infantry Division around 1900hrs.

US FORCES
A. Task Force A
B. 15th Cavalry
C. 17th Cavalry

8th Infantry Division
D. 13th Infantry
E. 28th Infantry
F. 121st Infantry
G. 2nd Rangers
H. FFI (Col. Eon)

With the breakout from Normandy, it appeared likely that Channel ports much nearer to the battlefield would soon be in Allied hands. On September 3, staff at Eisenhower's SHAEF (Supreme HQ Allied Expeditionary Force) recommended that plans to use Lorient, Quiberon Bay, Saint-Nazaire, and Nantes be abandoned; Eisenhower agreed on September 7. If the VIII Corps was not already committed to the capture of Brest, it was quite possible that its capture would have been cancelled. However, Eisenhower felt that Brest was an insurance policy in the event of a sudden change of fortune for the Allies. In the event, Marseilles on the Mediterranean was liberated on August 27, and the major port of Antwerp was captured on September 11, removing the need for the Brest port facilities.

An additional disincentive was the demolition of the Brest port. As at Cherbourg, the Kriegsmarine began a systematic program of demolition prior to the surrender to make the port unusable. All major wharfs, cranes, and other vital facilities were destroyer; channels were blocked with sunken ships. The city itself was a burned-out shell, largely due to Allied heavy bombing. Decisions later in September placed the rehabilitation of Brest at the lowest priority; later it was dropped altogether.

This left open the issue of the security of the other Breton ports. Lorient had a German garrison of about 25,000 and Saint-Nazaire a further 35,000. The forces there were mainly Kriegsmarine troops associated with the port. There was little evidence that these forces would sally forth. There were also several German fortified areas on the Bay of Biscay on either side of the Gironde estuary leading to Bordeaux. Elsewhere, there were two other significant *Festung* ports, the Channel Islands off the Breton coast, and Dunkirk on the Channel coast.

The 94th Infantry Division arrived in Europe on September 8, 1944 and was assigned to contain the remaining Breton ports. On arriving opposite Lorient and Saint-Nazaire, the division found that FFI Maquisards had already established a cordon around the ports, albeit badly organized and weakly armed. For more than a month, the 94th Infantry Division established

The French Armée de l'Atlantique staged Operation *Vénérable* on April 15–16, 1945 to liberate the port of Royan. Here, a column of Somua S-35 tanks of the 13e Regiment de Dragons is seen advancing in the Saint-Pierre sector. These tanks had been captured by the Germans from France in 1940, used in various campaigns in 1940–44, then taken back into French service during the containment of the *Festung* ports in 1944–45.

Hitler's last bastions, 1945

London

Portsmouth

Festung Dunkerque, May 9

Calais

Dunkirk

Plymouth

English Channel

Dieppe

Alderney

Cherbourg

Le Havre

Rouen

Guernsey

Channel Islands

Festung Kanalinseln, May 9

Jersey

Paris

Saint-Malo

Brest

Dinan

Rennes

Lorient

Festung Lorient, May 8

Vannes

Île de Groix

Angers

Tours

Quiberon

Belle-Île

Saint-Nazaire

Festung Saint-Nazaire, May 8

Nantes

Île de Noirmoutier

Île d'Yeu

Poitiers

Festung La Rochelle, May 8

Île de Ré

La Rochelle

Île d'Oléron

Rochefort

Bay of Biscay

Festung Royan, April 17

Royan

N

Bordeaux

0	100 miles
0	100km

The remaining *Festung* ports surrendered a day or two after the German capitulation at midnight on May 8–9, 1945. Here on May 7, Lt. Col. Erwin Gibson, executive officer of the 264th Infantry, 66th Infantry Division with his back to the camera, leads a US team to begin discussions with two German officers of the Festung Lorient garrison for the surrender. The actual surrender did not occur until the late morning of May 11, 1945.

patrols with the local FFI groups. In the case of the *Festung* ports on the Bay of Biscay, the FFI detachments were the only security force through the early autumn.

With most of France liberated, de Gaulle's provisional government had to decide on the future of the FFI. By August 1944, the FFI was estimated to number 400,000, although not all were armed. The FFI was a collection of local militias – some politically motivated, others more patriotically motivated. De Gaulle's government was aware that some of the most belligerent Maquis were those of the French communist party and there was some concern over their future political intentions. Regardless of the political threat, the immediate problem was the growing lawlessness in some areas, with the Maquis conducting retribution against collaborators. Order needed to be established or a civil war might ensue. The solution was two-fold. On the one hand, the 1ere Armée Française in Alsace needed reinforcements. This army had been raised from North African and West African colonial units, many of which had been in combat since early 1943. De Gaulle felt it was politically necessary to replace as many colonial troops as possible with Frenchmen, a process dubbed *"blanchissement"* (whitening). As a result, many FFI members were given the choice of being absorbed into the army or being disarmed and sent home. About 300,000 FFI members went to the army, and a further 40,000 to the French air force and navy.

The problem posed by the *Festung* ports on the Bay of Biscay provided an additional problem. The 1ere Armée Française in Alsace did not have sufficient divisions to send any back to the Atlantic coast for occupation duty. As a result, the idea emerged in October 1944 to use FFI units to create three new divisions that could be employed to cordon the *Festung* ports. Not surprisingly, two of these divisions were formed in Brittany due to the strong commitment of the local Breton Maquis. The 19e Division was formed under Gén. Henri Borgnis-Desbordes and the 25e Division under Gén. Raymond Chomel in Brittany. The third of these divisions, the 23e Division under Gén. André d'Anselme, was created in Charente. These units were equipped with older war-booty French equipment from 1940 still stored in German depots; some equipment such as tanks came from captured German equipment.

The mission to contain the Breton ports of Saint-Nazaire and Lorient eventually evolved into a joint Franco-American mission under the direction of Maj. Gen. Harry Maloney's 94th Infantry Division. By December 1944, there were 21 French battalions opposite the Breton ports, numbering 28,826 troops. During a truce in October 1944, the German garrisons expelled a large portion of the remaining French civilian population since there was a looming food shortage. There was some raiding by both sides during the autumn, the most dramatic of which was a German attack against the 2e Bataillon FFI de la Vienne near La Sicaudais on the southern end of the Saint-Nazaire pocket. This was mainly intended to secure the rich farmland there. The more battle-ready 8e Regiment de Cuirassiers was sent to the sector, putting an end to the German foray. The numerous German artillery units periodically harassed the FFI and US Army garrisons around the perimeter, and the Allied forces responded in kind. In December 1944, the 94th Infantry Division drove out the Germans from the villages of Erdeven, Étel, and Belz on the southeast side of the Étel Estuary to simplify the defense of position opposite Lorient.

By the end of 1944, there was a desperate shortage of infantry units in the US Army, and SHAEF decided to transfer the 94th Infantry Division to an active front. It was replaced on New Year's Day by the recently arrived 66th Infantry Division.

The *Festung* Ports 1944–45

Festung	Garrison (troops)	Commander	Surrender
Dunkirk	10,000	Vizeadmiral Friedrich Frisius	May 9, 1945
Channel Islands	28,500	Generalleutnant Rudolf Graf von Schmettow, Vizeadmiral Friedrich Hüffmeier	May 9, 1945
Lorient	26,000	General der Artillerie Wilhelm Fahrmbacher	May 10, 1945
Saint-Nazaire	30,000	Generalleutnant Hans Junck	May 11, 1945
La Rochelle	11,500	Vizeadmiral Ernst Schirlitz	May 9, 1945
Gironde Nord (Royan)	5,000	Konteradmiral Hans Michahelles	April 17, 1945
Gironde Süd (Le Verdon)	3,500	Oberst Otto Prahl	April 20, 1945

In late September 1944, De Gaulle decided to liberate the *Festung* ports once sufficient troops and equipment could be readied. Once the French Army became more fully organized in October 1944, De Gaulle assigned Gén. Edgar de Larminat to head the Atlantic front, which later became the Détachement d'Armée de l'Atlantique. French planning for the liberation of the *Festung* ports started with the smallest and weakest of the garrisons at Royan to be followed by the island of Oléron, La Rochelle, and finally Saint Nazaire. The initial plan for an attack on Royan, codenamed Operation *Independence*, was scheduled for late autumn 1944 but was canceled following the German attack in the Ardennes in December 1944 since Allied support for the French forces was no longer available. Nevertheless, there was a heavy RAF raid on Royan on January 5, 1945, largely as a preparation for the eventual mission. The Royan campaign was revived in the spring of 1945 under the new codename Operation *Vénérable*. The attack started with another large bombing raid on April 15, 1944, followed by an attack of the 23e Division, 2e Division Blindée and other French units. After two days of fighting, Vizeadmiral Michahelles surrendered the German garrison on April 17, 1945. This was followed by Operation *Jupiter* against Oléron Island, leading to the quick surrender on April 20, 1945. The battle for Royan was widely criticized within the French army, which felt that it was a prestige mission of little military value with the end of the war so near. There were plans to continue the reduction of the *Festung* ports with Operation *Musketeer* against La Rochelle, but the likelihood of an imminent German surrender and the heavy civilian casualties during the Royan fighting led to a cancellation of this plan along with associated plans for Lorient. The remaining ports were amongst the last German garrisons to surrender, in no small measure because they had lost contact with Berlin and did not know of the German capitulation until days later.

ANALYSIS

The battle for Brittany was one of the fastest campaigns by the Allies during the summer of 1944. The hilly *bocage* terrain might have been a defensive nightmare like the hedgerow country in the Saint-Lô area in July 1944. In the event, the German forces in Brittany had been so badly weakened by transfers to the Normandy front that the American advance was not seriously contested except at the ports. The strategic objective of the Brittany campaign was quickly abandoned once ports further east such as Antwerp were liberated in the late summer of 1944. The Brittany campaign might have been a sterile victory were it not for its under-appreciated role in dislodging the Kriegsmarine from the French Atlantic ports. This put a damper on Germany's U-boat campaign and permitted a resumption of normal shipping traffic on the southwestern approaches to the British Isles.

Field artillery played a vital role in the Brittany campaign, and especially during the battle for Brest. Both sides suffered from ammunition shortages. In the German case, the problem was not so much a lack of ammunition, but a very uneven supply of ammunition for the motley selection of weapons. Many of the weapons were war-booty types, especially French types from the 1940 campaign. The supplies of ammunition for these assorted types varied widely, but in a number of cases, field artillery ceased to be used once the limited ammunition supply was exhausted. In the case of other weapons, supplies were quite extensive. The Graf Spee battery was found to have ammunition supplies good "for months."

Another problem faced by the Wehrmacht was that a large portion of the guns were naval Flak weapons not suited to the field artillery role. As mentioned earlier, the Kriegsmarine Flak batteries were an essential element of the German defense lines. These weapons were widely used in a direct fire role, but they were not used extensively for traditional indirect fire field artillery missions such as counter-battery or harassing fire since the crews were not trained or equipped for this mission. Subsequent assessments by the US Army concluded that the defenders at Brest were hampered by the breakdown in artillery intelligence, inadequate forward observation, and problems with communication. An VIII Corps assessment concluded that German counter-battery fire against the US field artillery was "very ineffective." This was attributed to the fact that the German artillery was "devoid of flash and sound ranging apparatus and of air observation. Their efforts against our artillery were spasmodic and very ineffective."

The American infantry divisions that fought in the Brest campaign had endured the "Green Hell" of the hedgerow campaign in Normandy in June–July 1944 and were wary of enduring such high rates of casualties again. As a result, there was a tendency to use the rifle companies to fix the German defenses, and then destroy the German positions using field artillery. The main problem was a shortage of ammunition, especially in the period from August 29 to September 7. There was also a recurring shortage of certain ammunition types, especially smoke and white phosphorus. An VIII Corps assessment concluded that the rate of ammunition expenditure should have been about one unit of fire per day, but that ammunition shortages reduced this to less than half. The term "Unit of Fire" (U/F) refers to a standard number of rounds for specific type of gun based on expected expenditure in offensive or defensive missions. So for example, the unit of fire for the 105mm howitzer at the time was 130 rounds, while the unit of fire for the 240mm howitzer was 20. A summary of US Army field artillery ammunition expenditure is contained in the chart here.

VIII Corps Artillery Expenditure during the Battle for Brest

Type	No. of Guns	Rounds per gun per day	Total rounds	Total U/F	Avg. U/F per gun per day
105mm howitzer	138	78	270,493	15.0	0.6
155mm howitzer	85	43	91,547	14.6	0.59
155mm gun	24	31	18,618	14.8	0.59
155mm M12	24	15	9,955	8.6	0.34
4.5in. gun	24	25	14,861	9.0	0.36
8in. howitzer	24	19	11,528	9.8	0.39
240mm howitzer	12	11	3,153	14.0	0.56
8in. gun	12	6	1,608	3.9	0.15
90mm AA gun	16	51	2,248	3.1	1.0
3in. AT gun	108	15	40,870	7.8	0.3
76mm AT gun	48	11	13,747	5.7	0.23
Total (avg)	515	305 (28)	478,628	(9.7)	(0.46)

Due to the extensive number of forts, bunkers, and pillboxes, certain weapons proved unusually valuable in the fighting. The M10 3in. GMC and M18 76mm GMC tank destroyers were highly prized for direct fire against bunkers and armor steel structures such as armored bunker cupolas. These types of targets were almost impervious to field artillery even at pointblank range, but the tank destroyers were accurate enough to target view slits and embrasures. Each of the infantry divisions had an attached towed 3in. anti-tank gun battalion, but the self-propelled types were far more valuable in urban fighting due to their mobility and armored protection. However, they were in short supply and each division was generally allotted only a single company of these. The M12 155mm GMC was also highly prized for direct-fire missions for much the same reason, but these were allotted one at a time for only the most critical missions since there were only two battalions on hand. The 8in. howitzer was considered the most accurate weapon for destruction of pinpoint targets when used in an indirect fire mode. The 240mm howitzers proved to be especially well suited to attacks on the old forts when used with a time-delay fuze since the 360-pound projectile could penetrate through the outer masonry wall before the 50-pound high explosive charge detonated. Brest was one of the first campaigns when the new truck-mounted 4.5in. multiple rocket launcher was used. They were not popular due to their inaccuracy and dispersion compared to conventional field artillery.

In contrast to the vital role of artillery, there were many complaints about the shortcomings of air support in the campaign, especially tactical support in the final battles around Brest. Both the army and the USAAF expected greater results from the numbers of missions flown, but there was little understanding of the extent of German fortification around the city and the effect this had on dampening the effects of air strikes.

THE BATTLEFIELD TODAY

The ports of Saint-Malo and Brest were thoroughly destroyed during the war, but have been rebuilt in the years since the end of the war. Brittany is not on the usual tourist route due to its distance from the popular Normandy tourist circuit. Saint-Malo is more frequently visited than Brest due to its proximity to Mont Saint-Michel. As a result, there are far fewer museums devoted to the wartime experience.

There are extensive traces of the war both in the form of artifacts and memorials. Many Breton towns and villages have small plaques commemorating the events of 1944. The most extensive reminder of the war are the many surviving bunkers of the Atlantic Wall along the coast. These number in the several hundred, though many near the major cities and towns have been demolished or buried for the sake of convenience. The book by Patrick Bö listed below provides a detailed guide to some of the more scenic and best preserved bunkers, though hard-core bunker fanatics will want to get the Chazette books for more detailed coverage. When searching for bunkers, I have found that preparatory research is often necessary as the sites are seldom marked and are often away from major roads. The French IGN maps, especially the small scale 1: 12,500 maps for bicycling, sometimes show bunker locations under the rubric "*blockhaus ancienne.*" A search before traveling to the site using Google Earth is also an enormously useful tool.

For those visiting the two main Breton battlefields of 1944, the ever useful *After the Battle* magazine

The Château de la Duchesse Anne was the main German strongpoint within the walled town of Saint-Malo. It was badly damaged during the fighting and rebuilt after the war. It now serves as the town museum and the Hotel de Ville.

The Brittany American Cemetery is located in Saint James, about 12 miles (15km) south of Avranches. It contains the graves of 4,410 American military dead from the campaigns in Brittany and northern France. The cemetery and associated memorial chapel were completed in 1956. (American Battle Monuments Commission)

devoted two issues to these subjects, No. 33 (1981) covering Saint-Malo and No. 168 (2015) covering Brest. These provide an interesting comparison between iconic World War II images and their contemporary appearance, along with a handy summary of the campaigns. Back issues can be found through internet sources.

The main American military cemetery is located in Saint-Martin, immediately south of Avranches and not far from Saint-Malo. In the town of Saint-Malo, a "Memorial 39–5" was established in 1994 in the bunker of the air defense headquarters in the Fort de la Cité d'Alet, known as the Zitadelle by the Wehrmacht. Many of the sites associated with the battle are still visible around the town today, including the château, now the Hotel de Saint-Malo. From the walls of the town, Fort National and Cézembre are both visible out in the bay. The Musée de la Résistance Bretonne is devoted to the FFI movement in Brittany and is located in Saint-Marcel Malestroit near Vannes. Some of the sites in Brest such as the submarine pens are located on French Navy property and so are not easily accessible. There is a museum at Fort Montbarey to the west of Brest with displays dealing with its wartime history. Some of the Atlantic Wall sites in the area have also been turned into museums. For example, the Graf Spee fire control bunker at Kéromnès opened as a World War II museum in May 2017. Visitors should check with local tourism officials since the anniversaries of World War II have tended to lead to the creation of many new museums at historic sites.

Some of the sites in the countryside mentioned in this account can prove very difficult to find or may be inaccessible. For example, Hill 105 near Brest, fought over by the 23rd Infantry and II./FJR 7 in late August

1944, has been almost entirely submerged under recent construction. Hill 154 on the Amorique Peninsula is on private land and is almost entirely overgrown. A quarry has taken over much of Hill 103 near Plouzané. Another significant problem is that American accounts of the 1944 fighting were usually based on old GSGS maps that used different, and often incorrect, place names compared to contemporary maps. Battlefield tourism can be very interesting, but in less traveled areas such as Brittany, it requires far more preparation and research than in well-traveled areas such as Normandy.

FURTHER READING

The campaign in Brittany has remained obscure since it was overshadowed in the same timeframe by more dramatic campaigns such as the Falaise Pocket, the liberation of Paris, and the race to the German frontier. Coverage from the American perspective is much more thorough than from the German perspective. Besides published accounts of the US actions in Brittany, the author also consulted a variety of After-Action Reports (AAR) and the "Combat Interviews" collection in Records Group 407 at the US National Archives and Records Administration (NARA) in College Park, Maryland. Most German divisional records were lost during the fighting. Some 25. Armee Korps records can be found in Record Group 242 at NARA, but they largely end in July 1944 and have no coverage of the actual fighting. There are a few German accounts of the campaign in the US Army Foreign Military Studies (FMS) series. Some details about the conduct of the German defenses in Brest can be gleaned from the G2 periodic reports and prisoner of war interrogation reports of the US infantry divisions, and the author consulted those from the 2nd and 29th Infantry Divisions in Record Group 407 at NARA.

Unpublished reports and studies

Wayne Brame, et al., *Super Sixth in Exploitation (6th Armored Division: Normandy to Brest)* (Armored School, Fort Knox, 1949)

Wilhelm Fahrmbacher, *84 Corps and 25 Corps May 1942–10 May 1945*, (FMS B-731)

Maximilian Huenten, *Fortress Saint-Nazaire* (FMS A-980)

Rudolf Kogard, *343rd Infantry Division May–Sept 1944* (FMS B-427)

Commandant Rogé, *The FFI before and after D-Day* (FMS B-035)

Elliot Rosner, *The Jedburghs: Combat Operations in the Finistère Region of Brittany, France from July–September 1944* (Command and General Staff College, Ft. Leavenworth: 1990)

Robert Utley, *The Operations of Co. L, 38th Infantry (2nd Infantry Division) in Attack on Hill 154, Vicinity Brest France 22–23 Aug 1944* (The Infantry School, Fort Benning: 1950)

n.a. *Action at Fort Montbarey* (29th Infantry Division: 1945)

n.a. *Battalion and Small Unit Study No. 3: Brest* (ETO Historical Section 1945)

n.a. *Battalion and Small Unit Study No. 2: Fort Montbarey* (ETO Historical Section 1945)

n.a. *Defense of Brest: Forts-Strongpoints-Gun Positions*, (G-2 Section, 29th Infantry Division 1944)

n.a. *Report of the VIII Corps After Action Against Enemy Forces in Brittany* (VIII Corps, 1944)

n.a., *Report of the Artillery with the VIII Corps in the Reduction of Brest, 22 Aug–19 Sep 1944* (VIII Corps: 1944)

Articles

Alain Le Berre, "Bretagne été 1944: les renforts allemands tranferés en Normandie," *Magazine 39–45*, No. 290 July 2011; no. 291 August 2011; No. 292, Sep 2011.

Books

Balkoski, Joseph, *From Beachhead to Brittany: The 29th Infantry Division at Brest, August–September 1944* (Stackpole: 2008)

Blumenson, Martin, *US Army in WWII: Breakout and Pursuit* (US Army Center of Military History: 1961)

Bö, Patrick, *Le Mur de l'Atlantique en Bretagne* (Ed. Ouest-France: 2011)

Bougeard, Christian, *Histoire de la Résistance en Bretagne* (Ed.Jean-Aul Gisserot: 1992)

Braeuer, Luc, *Forteresse Saint-Nazaire: La marine allemande face aux Allies* (Imp. SPEI: 2002)

Braeuer, Luc, *L'incroyable histoire de la Poche de Saint-Nazaire* (Imp. SPEI: 2003)

Chazette, Alain, *Fallschirmjäger: les parachutists allemands en France 1943–44* (Histoire et Fortifications: 1999)

Chazette, Alain, Fabien Reberec, *Kriegsmarine: Mer du Nord, Manche, Atlantique 1940–45* (Heimdal: 1997)

Chazette, Alain, et al, *Atlantikwall: Mythe ou Réalité* (Histoire et Fortifications: 2008)

Rémy Desquesnes, *Les poches de résistance allemandes sur le littoral français: Août 1944–mai 1945* (Ed. Ouest-France: 2011, 2017)

Chazette, Alain, et al., *Forteresse de Brest: La région de Saint-Renan* (Histoire et Fortifications: 2014)

Ewing, Joseph, *29 Let's Go! A History of the 29th Infantry Division in World War II* (Infantry Journal Press: 1948)

Floch, Henri, Alain Le Berre, *L'Enfer de Brest* (Heimdal: 2001)

Gaujac, Paul, *Special Forces in the Invasion of France* (Histoire & Collections: 1999)

Gawne, Jonathan, *The Battle for Brest: The Americans in Brittany 1944* (Histoire & Collections: 2002)

Hofmann, George, *The Super Sixth: History of the 6th Armored Division in World War II* (6th Armored Division Association: 1975)

Jones, Benjamin, *Eisenhower's Guerillas: The Jedburghs, the Maquis & the Liberation of France* (Oxford Univeristy Press: 2016)

Kammann, Willi, *Der Weg der 2.Fallschirmjäger-Division* (Schild-Verlag: 1972)

Lamarque, Philippe, *Bretagne: Brest dans la guerre* (Editions CMD: 1999)

Ramcke, Hermann, *Fallschirmjäger: Brest and Beyond 1944–51* (Shelfbooks: 2016)

Sakkers, Hans, *Festung St. Malo: Een eindstrijd tot het uiterste 5 aug- 2 sept 1944* (Koudekerke: 2001)

n.a., *Combat History of the 2nd Infantry Division in World War II* (Germany, 1946; republished by Battery Press, 2001)

n.a. , *Combat History of the 6th Armored Division in the European Theater of Operations 18 July 1944-8 May 1945* (Ripple Publishing: 1946)

n.a, *Conquer: The Story of the Ninth Army 1944–45* (Infantry Journal Press: 1947)

INDEX

References to images are in **bold**.